INSIDE MY HEART

INSIDE MY HEART

Choosing to Live with Passion and Purpose

ROBIN MCGRAW

NELSON BOOKS
A Division of Thomas Nelson Publishers
Since 1798

www.thomasnelson.com

Published in Nashville, Tennessee, by Thomas Nelson, Inc.

Nelson Books titles may be purchased in bulk for educational, business, fund-raising, or
sales promotional use. For information, please e-mail SpecialMarkets@ThomasNelson.com.

Library of Congress Cataloging-in-Publication Data

McGraw, Robin.
  Inside my heart : choosing to live with passion and purpose / Robin
McGraw.
      p. cm.
  ISBN 0-7852-1836-X (hardcover)
  ISBN 0-7852-8856-2 (IE)
  1. Christian women—Religious life. I. Title.

  BV4527.M3923 2006
  248.8'43—dc22

2006019830

Printed in the United States of America

2 3 4 5 6 RRD 09 08 07 06

To my loving husband and best friend, Phillip.
I have loved you from the moment God brought us together.

and to

My sons, Jay Phillip and Jordan Stevens,
I love you boys so much. You are my passion.
You are my purpose.

and to

My mother, Georgia, for teaching me to walk with grace
and dignity on the good days and the bad. And to my father,
Jim, for overcoming more than a man should face and
loving me so well along the way.

and to

All women out there embracing the choices of life.

CONTENTS

ACKNOWLEDGMENTS

I chose the title, *Inside My Heart*, because the writing of this book was definitely a "feeling" rather than thinking experience. At 52 years of age I feel that despite some difficult times along the way, I have absolutely, positively got to be one of the most blessed women in the world. I choose the word *blessed*, rather than *lucky*, because I believe that God has personally watched over me, every step of the way, each and every day. "Acknowledgment" of His grace is not a big enough word to describe those blessings.

Greatest among those blessings has got to be my husband, Phillip. He has loved me, believed in me, supported me and lifted me up from the minute we met. From the very second I felt his strong arms around me I knew I had found the man God had chosen for me to spend my life with. When I decided to write this book, he was absolutely thrilled. Being an accomplished author he knew how much work it would be yet had no doubt that I could and would see it through. He calls himself my "cautious critic" because he knows that I hate being told what to do. So it was with great courage and personal peril that he gave me not only love and support, but constructive criticism along the way. Phillip, you have always been next to me publicly and inside my heart privately. I thank you for being the one that claps and cheers the loudest in my life each and every day. Our journey has just begun.

Thanks also to my dear family, Jordan and Jay, and now my precious new daughter-in-law, Erica. You boys are the greatest source of joy I as a mother could ever imagine. You will find yourselves throughout these pages, because you have been my mission in life. Watching you turn into the young men you have become gives me the strength, courage and confidence to write this book and share experiences of my life and our family with so many people around the world. Every time I looked at or thought about you two, I wrote faster and more furiously to inspire women to be simply the best they can be in hopes that they would have the rewards of the heart that I reap when I look at you. Thank you both for your help, support and love during this long process. If not another thing happens in my life the two of you have made the journey more than any woman or mother could ask.

Thanks also to my sisters, Jamie, Cindi, and Karin, and to Roger my twin brother. So many of the lessons that I have learned and shared in this book were experienced with each of you at my side. All four of you always made me feel so completely special and

I know it was hard on you, knowing that I was mother and daddy's favorite! HA!

Thanks also to Phillip's sisters Deana, Donna and Brenda. Sometimes I think you three taught him too much about women, because I'll be darned if I could ever get away with anything! Seriously, you three have been my staunch supporters since my first date with your brother and have always treated me like family, which at times was so desperately important. Thanks for all you have been over the last thirty-five years.

A very special thanks to "Grandma Jerry" for being my "other mother," particularly because I lost my mother so early on. Having such a rich and wonderful relationship with you has meant more to me and has filled a greater void than you could ever know. Your loving and caring spirit, always upbeat attitude and relentless courage in the face of amazing pain and challenge in your own life has inspired me to be a better woman. Thank you most for the gift of the wonderful man you raised and gave to me with such uncon-ditional blessing. You have been a mother first and a mother-in-law second and a champion at both. Grandma, thank you for loving me, and our little family.

I also have to thank Scott Madsen, family member, friend, sup-porter, and world-class giver. Scott you've never said no, are never too tired to help out and always find a positive way to contribute. Your help and support while writing this book and assistance with the logistics have been invaluable. Thanks for always being there.

A special thanks also to my good friend Jan Davidson. Jan, you and I grew together as women, mothers and wives over the last twenty years. Everything we have shared, whether it is trials and tribulations or exciting adventures and victories simply would not have been the same without you by my side. You were there for so many of the things I've shared in this book and I am so thankful that you were. It is so great to have a friend that always unfailingly revels in your successes and wishes you nothing but the best. Thanks for always being there, and I can't wait to see what the next twenty years brings to our lives.

A special thanks to Terry Wood and Carla Pennington. Although I have only known you two for the last five years, you have both shared and contributed so much to this little behind-the-scenes "country girl" finding her away through the maze of the public eye. Your belief in me, constant coaching and support helped me to find the right note for taking my voice, beliefs and values public. We have laughed and cried, but have definitely made a difference. Nobody could ever ask for better girlfriends. Thanks for being exactly who you are.

Thanks to Robin Cantor-Cooke for your warm, conscientious, professional contribution to this book. You are one of the hardest working mothers I have ever met: the way you balance your family and work inspires everyone who meets you.

To my agents, Jan Miller and Shannon Miser-Marven, and the dedicated and talented team at Dupree/Miller & Associates, this book would not be a reality without you, your belief in me, and your long hours of diligent work and editing. Your passionate commitment to getting this book into the hands of every woman in America has made such a huge difference. First, thank you both for being such good friends, and second, for being such cutting-edge, devoted and caring professionals. You are the best.

To Mary Graham and the Women of Faith organization, thank you for giving me your stage to voice my message with tens of thousands of listening women. Your organization is dedicated to touching the hearts of so many women, and I am honored to be a part of your family.

And from the bottom of heart, I want to say thank you to Thomas Nelson Publishing. To Jonathan Merkh, who embraced my vision for this book from day one and whose support never wavered, and to Mike Hyatt for caring so much about this book. Thank you to the tremendously talented and gifted team at Thomas Nelson. You all made this a world-class publishing experience.

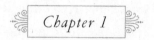

Chapter 1

FROM MY HEART
TO YOURS

I am on a mission to get you excited about your life. And let me tell you, I'm excited—not only excited to be a woman, but to be a wife, a mother, an enthusiastic homemaker, and embarking on a new career as an author at the age of fifty-two. My greatest hope is that what I put down in these pages may inspire and help you and other women by offering an honest look inside at who I am: how I've lived my life, the struggles I've faced, the decisions I've made, and how I've made them. The journey hasn't always been easy and it sure hasn't always been fun, and I've had my share of disappointments along the way.

I believe I'm smarter today than I was yesterday, and I know I'm a whole lot smarter than I was ten, twenty, or thirty years ago. I'm smart enough now to value the experiences I've had over the half-century I've been in this world, and I know that the ones that count are all a result of the choices I've made. But I also know that many people aren't aware that there *are* choices to be made, that they *do* have control over a lot of what happens to them. The freedom to choose the way we live our lives is one of the great gifts we've been given, and that's what I'm going to talk about in this book.

> You can make choices in your life; in fact, you *must* make choices in order to have the life you want. And whether or not you're aware of it, you *do* make choices all the time; even choosing not to choose is a choice. I know this is the truth because it's a truth I have lived.

A lot of people go through life without really thinking about who they are or why they do the things they do. It's as if we're living on autopilot, staring straight ahead without seeing anything other than what's right in front of our faces. I know what this feels like because it's happened to me. I'm usually able to snap out of my daze and get back in control pretty quickly, but I know how easy it is to go passive. We do things or agree to things or accept whatever comes things or accept whatever comes our way without considering whether or not it's right for us. And by passively accepting whatever happens, we give up chances every day to create the lives we want.

It doesn't have to be that way. You can make choices in your life; in fact, you *must* make choices in order to have the life you want. And whether or not you're aware of it, you *do* make choices all the time; even choosing not to choose is a choice. I know this is a truth because it's a truth I have lived.

In my heart, I've always known what I wanted, ever since I was a little girl. I live every day of my life as an adventure, and I approach every aspect of my life as an event. Life has tried to knock that spirit out of me, and you probably know what that feels like. But I always have faith that things will get better. And it doesn't matter how old I get; I still wake up every morning grateful to be alive and healthy, and passionate about making the most of the day. And while I've always known this about myself, it wasn't until I sat down to write this book that I thought about how I got that way, and how it is that my life turned out the way it has. I simply cannot imagine wanting to be anything or anyone other than who I am: a freethinking woman, wife of the man I love, and mother of two grown sons.

Notice I said "grown sons." When my younger son left for college a year ago, I declared my independence from the rigors of daily parenting and am now poised on the brink of a new and exciting phase of life. I don't know if fifty is the new thirty, but I do know that I'm in my fifties now and I love it. I also know that I didn't become who I am through dumb luck; I did it by listening to God's voice, knowing myself, and using all of that knowledge to create the life I wanted.

You see, I absolutely believe that in order for a woman to experience happiness, fulfillment, and peace, she needs to know

> I absolutely believe that in order for a woman to experience happiness, fulfillment, and peace, she needs to know two things: who she is, and who she is *meant* to be.

two things: who she is, and who she is *meant* to be. They're not quite the same thing: the first one has to do with the reality of your life, and the second one has to do with your purpose for being in this world, which is something each of us has to discover for herself and cannot be dictated by any other person in our lives—not by our husbands, parents, children, employers, or friends.

I think it's getting harder and harder to tell the difference between who we are and who we're meant to be. So much of the time, we lose ourselves just trying to keep up with the frantic pace of life. We drag ourselves out of bed in the morning, already half an hour behind, and spend much of the day responding to the needs and demands of others. Somewhere along the line, we often lose track of the essential feminine self—that unique, life-giving entity that invigorates our beings and warms the souls of the people we love.

I want to get you excited about whatever phase of life you're in, excited about being a woman in this day and time, excited about being the woman that God created you to be.

But we don't have to lose that feminine self, and the way to hold on to her is to accept nothing less than being simply the best—the best we can be in the roles we choose for ourselves: wife, mother, daughter, sister, and friend. And when it comes to mothers, there's something I want to say: whether you stay at home with your children or work a job and then come home to your children, the point is, you're still a full-time mother, and beyond that, a woman. We were women long before

4

we were mothers, and we'll be women long after our children leave the nest.

I believe we were put on this earth to enjoy lives of joy and abundance, and that is what I want for you and for me. I want to get you excited about whatever phase of life you're in, excited about being a woman in this day and time, excited about being the woman that God created you to be.

And it's all there for the choosing, because I believe in the core of my soul that how you live, how I live, how we all live as women is largely a matter of choice. We have the right to choose to be happy. We have the right to choose to have a good attitude. It's all a choice. And I'll tell you right now, I am going to use that word a lot in this book, because choice is very important to me.

A lot of women hear me say this, and I imagine a lot of them may think, *That's easy for you to say. You live in a wonderful house with a successful man who loves you, and you can probably have anything you want—you're a privileged person.* And all that is true. But do you know what the real privilege is? The real privilege is being free to embrace the joyful aspects of life and reject the hurtful ones, to choose to do what's working, and to turn your back on what isn't. It's a privilege to have the right to take charge of your existence and be excited about your life.

You don't need a lot of costly stuff to be happy: our first apartment was a whopping 420 square feet of linoleum and worn nylon pile, and I used to drive a 1962 Comet with bright turquoise paint that looked as if it had been brushed on. I lived the first forty-eight years of my life in the heartland of this country, and when I was a

kid, the only spoons I had in my mouth were stainless steel, not silver. Still, I always felt fortunate to be who I was, and excited by the
prospect of what life held for me.

I chose to make my husband and my children the center of my
life, and I've never regretted that for a moment—not one single second. Ever since I was a little girl, I knew that I was put on this earth
to be a wife and a mother, and that's exactly what I chose to do.
And it is through the integrity of that choice that I have created the
life I longed for and never had when I was a child.

I grew up in Oklahoma with three older sisters, a twin brother,
and parents who loved us with all their hearts. They were also crazy
about each other, which went a long way toward teaching us kids
how a man and woman could live together in a small house, raise
five children, and still get along. We never had enough money to
buy everything we wanted or needed, yet we always thought of ourselves as loved rather than deprived.

My father was a binge-drinking alcoholic and an addicted gam-
bler. Because of that I lived every day in uncertainty. I woke up
every morning thinking, *Did daddy come home last night?* And, if
he hadn't, *Is this the day he'll come home?* Or if he had been
around consistently for a while, I'd wonder, *Is this the day this man
I love so much will start drinking and gambling again? How long
will this binge last? Will there be enough money to buy food? Will
the electric company cut off the lights again this month? How long
will it be before he's back at work during the day and comes home
at night and acts like my dad again?*

I knew he was a good and wonderful man and I loved him with

all my heart. I also knew he had an illness that cheated my sisters, my brother, and me out of the father we yearned for. When I was just a little girl, I wanted more than anything to make my father well. But because I couldn't do that, I decided that I would dedicate my life to undoing the legacy of doubt, pain, fear, and uncertainty that accompanied his great love for us. I forgave him even then, when I was little, but the fear never left.

So when I grew up, my plan was to fall in love, get married, and start my own family. And I decided then and there that I would not bring that part of my father's legacy into my adult life. I would never marry or even date a man who drank or gambled. I can remember making a conscious choice and telling myself: I adore my father and I am going to bring every good part of his legacy into my life and live it and embrace it in my husband and in my children. But I will not allow that part of his legacy into my adult life.

If my father had a powerful influence on me, so did the extraordinary woman who was my mother. To put it simply, my mother lived for her children. She always put herself last. If there wasn't quite enough food for dinner, she was the one who didn't get a full plate. She'd often be up well past midnight, scrubbing the bathroom floor or ironing my father's shirts or sitting hunched over her sewing machine, making me a skirt or a blouse out of remnants she'd gotten on sale.

And then there were the nights she'd drive around town with me or one of my siblings in the car, looking for my father, who hadn't been home in a couple of days. We'd drive slowly with the windows rolled down, peering down side streets to see if my father was lying unconscious in a deserted parking lot or dead in an alleyway. We went out on a number of those gloomy excursions but we never would find him. She'd always drive home tired but grimly optimistic that he'd turn up alive and relatively well before too long.

That precious woman never put herself first. She also never took care of herself, which is why she died of a catastrophic heart attack at the age of fifty-eight—just six years older than I am now. I was married and the mother of a six-year-old son when she died, and I swore to myself that day that I would never allow myself to become so drained and depleted. I loved my mother and I have carried her legacy of love and devotion into my relationship with my children. But I have also chosen to reject the legacy of self-neglect that caused her to be taken from me when I still needed her so much. That is why I eat healthy food, exercise every day, and make sure I take care of myself so my body doesn't fall apart before it has to. That's exactly what my mother would have wanted for me, even if she didn't do it for herself. I truly believe that I can best honor my mother's memory not by perpetuating her legacy but by choosing the parts of it that are right for me, and losing the ones that aren't.

The concept of redefining your legacy is something I am passionate about, especially when it comes to women, many of whom are merely existing inside lives they neither chose nor contemplated. So many of us have dutifully reproduced our mother's or father's behaviors, duplicating our parents' patterns and manifesting a legacy that we, however unconsciously, feel obligated to fulfill.

I want you to know you have a choice: you do not have to haul your parents' legacy into your life like that old dining room set your great aunt left you in her will. If it makes you happy to eat at that table and sit in those chairs, by all means keep them. But if it doesn't, remember: you have options. You can hold on to the table and toss the chairs. Or lose the table and keep the chairs (perhaps reupholster the seats so they're more comfortable). And if you just plain hate the whole thing, get rid of it before you bring it into the house.

Just as your great aunt's furniture might not suit your dining room, your parents' ways of living might not suit your life. You're not insulting your dead aunt by rejecting her old furniture, and you're not betraying your parents by living your life differently than they lived theirs; in fact, what you're doing is being true to yourself. I believe in the core of my being that you don't have to bring into your life anything that isn't working for you, nor are you fated to live out a future you had no part in creating. Each of us possesses the will to create her own legacy. It's all a choice.

Writing this book has required me to think about the choices I've made, and it has made me aware of the exhilarating power of living a life of my own choosing. I don't know how it happened, but as far back as I can remember, I've always known my life had a purpose, and I've pursued that purpose with a passion. I have never thought of myself as a victim of circumstance; rather, I examined the circumstances I was in, evaluated their usefulness in my life, and used them as a blueprint for how I would build the life I wanted. I always pictured myself as the one person and the only force besides God who I could count on to design the life I wanted to live, and make it a reality. I knew I was meant to be a wife and mother, and I made it happen. I wanted a husband who didn't drink or gamble, and I made it happen. I wanted to take care of myself to remain vibrant and healthy for my family; and I made it happen (although I confess that the day I get rid of the treadmill just might be the happiest day of my life). And everything that has happened is the result of conscious choices that I made—some of which, I must tell you, were difficult to make and scary to live with. The bottom line, though, was that the thought of living a life I didn't want was much, much scarier than taking responsibility for choosing to create the life I did want.

> My goal for this book is to tell everyone who reads it about the power of choosing her life rather than taking it as it comes along—not so you'll make the same choices I made, but so you can make the choices that are right for *you*.

I believe that in this life, we are defined not by the station in life into which we are born, nor by our pedigree, race, or religion, but by the choices we make. By choosing to live with passion and purpose, I have fashioned a rich and rewarding life—not because I'm special, or a genius, or born under a lucky star. Far from it: I grew up poor and was raised by uneducated parents. We were blue-collar and sometimes no-collar, and it wasn't unusual for us to have cold cereal for dinner.

I never had a store-bought dress until I was out of high school, and I was forced to adapt to life in a household where you were never really sure who was in charge.

But I always went to bed knowing that my parents loved me, and knowing that someday I would use that love to warm the hearts of my own children. It was then, when I

> I believe that in this life, we are defined not by the station in life into which we are born, nor by our pedigree, race, or religion, but by the choices we make.

was just a girl in Duncan, Oklahoma, that I made a choice to be the best that I could be, and I am living proof of the wisdom of that choice.

My goal for this book is to tell everyone who reads it about the power of choosing her life rather than taking it as it comes along—not so you'll make the same choices I made, but so you can make the choices that are right for *you*. I'm certainly not an expert on your life, but I *am* an expert on mine, and that is what I hope to share with you.

It's not my intention to give people advice on how to solve their problems (I leave that to my husband). But I've had my share of struggles over the years, and I know a thing or two about what has worked for me in this life. I have learned which battles to pick, when and how to push back, and how to bend without breaking. In short, I have figured out how not to lose "me" in the course of being so many things to so many people in so many areas of my life. I have

chosen to be an active participant in my life rather than a specta-
tor, and in so doing I have chosen how to be a woman, how to be
a wife, and how to be a mother in ways that are uniquely my own.
I offer the stories of these choices as evidence of the power of sheer
determination, will, and faith in God.

To be sure, I'm not doing it alone. I wake up every morning and
I thank God for everything that is good, right, and true in my life.
I am thankful for a husband who has placed me in the forefront of
his heart because I've chosen to stand beside him. I am thankful for
two fine, strong sons who remind me every day of the rightness of
my mission here on earth. I am thankful for all the people in my
life whose love and care are sources of constant rejuvenation for
my spirit. Finally, I am thankful for the gift of free will and for the
chance to choose the life God means for me to lead.

Not least, I am thankful for the opportunity to reach out to
women everywhere, and touch their lives by telling them about
mine. I want to reach out to all women—older and younger, married and single, women who are mothers and those who are not,
women who work outside the home and those who don't.

As I write this book, I find myself looking deeply into the reser-
voir of memory and seeing reflections of things I haven't thought
about in years, sometimes decades. When I reach out to touch
them, I do so gently. God has blessed me so that I can still feel the
touch of my mother's hand and see my father's smile. This is what
I offer, with equal parts humility, wonder, and truth. Should any of
it touch anyone, anywhere, in any way, I shall consider myself
abundantly blessed.

Chapter 2

A Woman's Heart (and Mind)

If you're married, a lot of your time and energy goes into living with your husband. Sometimes it's easy, sometimes it's hard, and sometimes it's impossible. I have been living with my husband for over thirty years now, and I have to say it's better than any dream I ever had. Still, people do ask me all the time what it's like to live with Dr. Phil. Just in case you're wondering the same thing, I'll tell you what I tell them: I don't live with Dr. Phil; I live with a man.

It's true that the man I live with is "America's therapist," as he's sometimes called, but at home he is just like any other husband: he's a man, with all the lovable and quirky qualities that implies. When it comes to figuring things out, it seems as though Phillip always has the answer, especially when it involves people and what makes them tick. That's great, but also frustrating sometimes. Every once in a while I tell him, "Honey, I don't want to know what you think; I want to be emotional, irrational, and impulsive!"

Seriously, though, I'm also right a lot of the time; and when I am, I'm not shy about saying so. I never hesitate to speak up when I believe I'm not being taken seriously by doctors, contractors, teachers, principals, or America's therapist, for that matter. After all, we're talking about a man who will argue with the dog as though he expects a rational response. (As a matter of fact, yes honey, sometimes you do have "stupid" stamped on your forehead.) We tease each other a lot, but the fact of the matter is he never comes close to being stupid, even when he is wrong; and when that happens, it isn't as much that he's wrong as that he's a man.

Here's an example. This happened about a year ago, not long after Jordan left for college. It was one of those nights when the house seemed too quiet; I was really missing the sound of Jordan's voice echoing from the upstairs landing, "Mom, I'm hungry!" I was missing the "Grand Central Station" activity of all his friends, and his rock band's seemingly endless rehearsals. I remembered the house-is-too-quiet feeling from seven years earlier, when Jay left for school. But Jordan was only eleven then, and I still had plenty of science projects, baseball games, and erupting laundry hampers to look forward to. But now Jordan was gone, too, and the shape of my life had changed.

I'd had ample time to prepare for Jordan's departure—some eighteen years' worth (I think every mother starts anticipating her kids' leaving from the moment they arrive.)—and it wasn't as if I had nothing to fill my time. Between tapings of my husband's television show (I'm in the audience every day, and participate in many of the shows dealing with women's issues), conducting my own projects (such as being ambassador for the Dr. Phil Foundation's work with disadvantaged children), and responding to what seems like millions of e-mails, I don't have time to sit around moping and missing my kids.

Moreover, I had promised myself I would not get all weepy around Jordan during his last few weeks at home because I never wanted him to feel sad or guilty about what he was about to do with his life. I'd been relentlessly cheerful as I helped him track down extra-long sheets for his dorm-room bed and made sure he packed enough soap and shampoo. True, I'd had a few close calls, especially when he'd come over and hug me and I could not keep myself from thinking, *Robin, remember what this feels like, because you might not feel it again until Thanksgiving.* What I definitely felt was an ache in my chest and a rising tide behind my eyelids.

But I had been strong and held it together when Jordan was around. After all, I was happy he was going off to college and pleased that he'd been accepted by Southern Methodist University, his brother's law school alma mater, even if it was two time zones away from Los Angeles, where we are living now. Nothing was more important to me than being a good mother to my sons, and I figured I was doing all right if my youngest felt confident enough to go off and live one thousand, two-hundred-thirty-seven-point-one-three miles, more or less, away from his dad and me. But this was one of those nights when, if I thought about Jordan, my heart would lurch and I'd end up crying in bed, bath, and way beyond.

The lights were out, Phillip had dozed off, and I was lying next to him, converting my pillow into a swamp. He didn't say anything, but he must have heard me sniffling because he rolled over and took me in his arms and started patting me. And I thought, *Oh, bless his heart, I woke him up, and now he knows I'm crying so he's comforting me.* And he just lay there with his arms around me, patting my shoulder, and I started to feel better. So I finally got up and went to the bathroom and washed my face. I was on my way back to the bed when it hit me. I stopped right there in my bare feet.

"Wait just a minute," I said. "What good are you? Here I am, all upset, and you just go stupid on me!"

Now he was wide awake.

"What are you talking about?" he said.

"Not a word! You pat me on the arm, and that's it? Where are all those words of wisdom you usually have?"

The man just stared at me.

"You're Dr. Phil!" I said. "I'm married to Dr. Phil, and that's *it*? You don't have a single thing to say to me!" But of course, never at a loss, he did.

"You're always telling me that I don't have to fix everything," he said. "You're the one who says that sometimes I just have to be there for you and hold you."

He was right. I had told him that maybe ten thousand times, which made it even worse.

"Isn't that just like a man," I said, "to take my words and use them on me!"

So that's what I mean when I say I don't live with Dr. Phil, I live with a man—a man who, according to the *New York Times*, is the nation's most visible self-help specialist and relationship guru, but who is still a *man*. A man who loves and knows me better than anyone else on earth, but who still can't read my mind (at least not all the time).

And why shouldn't Phillip be just like a man? He is a man, after all: my one and only love, the man God meant me to marry; the father of my children and my husband of over thirty years. I met him, fell for him, and married him long before he was who he is today, and yet he hasn't changed, not on the inside. He was Phillip McGraw when I met him, and then he was Dr. McGraw, and for the last nine years he's been Dr. Phil, but to me he's always been a sweet, funny man who took the feeling of being truly loved to a whole new level.

From our very first date—during which I did *not* mention marriage, by the way, no matter what *he* says—I have always thought that he was brilliant. To this day, I totally trust his opinion, and respect his mind and who he is. But when he comes home at night after a long day of taping at the studio, hungry and tired and wondering what's for dinner, he is most certainly not Dr. Phil. In all the years we've been married, he has never asked me how something's working for me, or looked at me as if I were crazy and said, "Now, what in the world were you thinking?"

He knows better than that. He knows that if I want Dr. Phil, I will ask for him. Phillip has a big personality. He's strong, he's assertive, and for a long time he was one of three men living in our house. I knew early on, as the only woman in this family, that I was going to have to stake out my territory, my boundaries, my wants, and my needs, or I could get swept away in a house full of jocks. As I said, it's all about choices, and I made the choice to be sure that I had a strong and clear voice that was heard, and that I was treated with dignity and respect by all three of the men in my life.

Having said that, I will admit that it's great to have Dr. Phil at my beck and call. I'm always coming up to him and saying, "Gosh, that person is so, so . . . give me a word. Give me a word." And that means, "Give me Dr. Phil." He can sum up an emotion or an event or anything for me, really, in one or two syllables, and that's all I need.

> As I said, it's all about choices, and I made the choice to be sure that I had a strong and clear voice that was heard, and that I was treated with dignity and respect by all three of the men in my life.

I'll say, "Oh, that person! She's so . . . so . . ." And he'll look up without missing a beat and say, "Self-involved?" And I'll jump up and say, "Perfect, perfect." Whenever a situation or a person frustrates me, Dr. Phil can sum it up. So sure, he can be Dr. Phil when I need him to be. But he doesn't give me that side of him unless I ask for it.

One time when we were newlyweds living in a little apartment outside of Dallas, way before he was Dr. Phil but when he was already a psychologist, I asked one too many questions. I was working during the day and going to college at night, and Phillip was working on his doctorate at the University of North Texas. We were both at home studying, and Phillip was working to perfect the skill of performing psychological assessments on patients. I said, "Do you want to practice on me?" (In retrospect, that qualified me as an idiot. He might have discovered my shoe obsession and headed for the hills!)

He said he was going to ask me a lot of questions that I had to answer as honestly as I could, and I figured, how hard can it be? I'm married to the man, after all; he knows everything about me. So he started doing the profile and I started squirming. He asked me all these questions about my mother and my father, and how I felt about my brother and my sisters, and he wrote everything down. The more questions he asked, the more I found myself stammering and stalling for time, and I was getting so nervous I finally got up on my tip-toes and looked him right in the eye and said, "Now, listen buddy—this assessment is over." It was dawning on me what all this man was learning. I said, "Okay, I know I said I'd do this with you, but don't you be using this test on me, and don't you be analyzing me when I don't know it. If you're going to analyze me, it'll be when I ask you to." I set that rule down way back.

I never again asked Phillip to analyze me or my behaviors the way he would do for a patient. I guess it's similar to the way surgeons aren't supposed to operate on family members because they might be too emotionally involved to use their best medical judgment. And while doing brain surgery on your wife is a lot different from trying to get inside her head with a psychological profile, the whole thing was still a little too close for my comfort level.

I remember another time, many years later, when we were sitting in the car after one of Jordan's baseball games, waiting for him to come out of the locker room. The parents' cars were all lined up, waiting for the kids, and the mothers were all lined up in the courtyard, talking and laughing and visiting. Now, I like a good chat as much as the next girl, but I'd just spent two hours visiting with these women during the game, and at this point, I just wanted to sit in my car with my husband, mind my own business, and wait for my son to appear so we could all go home and have dinner.

I turned to Phillip (huge mistake) and said something like, "I wonder what it is about me that I have no desire to join those women and continue visiting. Do you think that's a bad thing?"

Now, what he should have said was, "Oh, no, honey, that's not a bad thing; there's not a bad thing about you—you're perfect!"

What he actually said was, "Well, yes, it could mean that you have antisocial tendencies and are trying to avoid interpersonal contact with members of your peer group."

I just looked at him and thought, *Oh, my gosh. Is he really that dense, thinking he can tell me what all's wrong with me like that? Doesn't he know me any better than that after twenty-three years, seven months, and three weeks of marriage?* It made me so mad I didn't talk to him for hours. I kept replaying it in my head: him sitting there in the driver's seat, giving me this insight into myself, and me sitting there saying, "Gosh, Phillip, did you have to say that?" What he'd said wasn't exactly derogatory, but it wasn't a compliment, either. I just didn't like the way it sounded.

I was mad at him for the rest of the night—and I mean the you-sit-over-there-on-the-couch-and-I'll-sit-by-myself-in-this-chair kind of mad (because I'm so antisocial, don't you know). Poor man, he sat there shaking his head and muttering, "Well, you asked me." And I was all hurt and huffy, saying, "Well yeah, but—you know." He didn't know, of course. He's a man, and when you tell a man you want him to tell you the truth, he thinks you mean it. And I sort of did, but I didn't want him seeing me in those terms, as if I were a research subject that he could poke at and figure out. He was my husband, not my therapist. I never asked him to explain myself to me again.

It works for us to maintain a boundary between what he does for a living and how we live our lives at home. I'm not married to that man in a conservative suit and tie who helps people with their problems on national television. I am married to Phillip McGraw, Grandma's son. That's what we all call his mother and that's how I see him, the son of a woman who did an outstanding job raising a fine and decent man, just the way I've tried to do with our sons. And if I've done half as good a job with my kids as Grandma did with hers, I'll be able to look back on my life and feel good about myself.

> I have always felt that motherhood was my calling, and I have always known I am going to do everything I can for my children because I want to be able to say that I'm doing a good job, with no regrets.

That's important to me, because as I said earlier, I believe I was put on this earth to be not only a wife and a mother, but to be Phillip's wife and Jay and Jordan's mother, and I really just want to be able to look back on my family—my life's work— and know that I did a good job. I have always felt that motherhood was my calling, and I have always known I am going to do everything I can for my children because I want to be able to say that I'm doing a good job, with no regrets.

I want to be proud of myself because I raised decent children. I do not ever want to live with the regret of knowing I could have tried a little harder to help my kids become happy, healthy adults. That doesn't mean I couldn't have done things better or differently. As a young bride and mother, I made all the predictable, typical mistakes and then some. I still cannot believe that I did what I am about to tell you. Talk about a clueless new mother—I defined the term. Okay, here goes.

I brought Jay home from the hospital, placed him in his crib with color-coordinated sheets, blanket, and bumper pads, and realized I didn't have any diapers, bottles, or baby formula in the house. (Heck, I'd only had nine months to prepare, and I was busy decorating the nursery, you know?) So I went to the bag of supplies the hospital sent home with us, fished out the baby bottle and the can of formula, diluted the formula with a can of water the way the hospital nurse had told me to, poured it into the bottle, heated the bottle in a pan of water on the stove, and gave baby Jay his very first home-cooked meal.

In the meantime, I asked Phillip to run to the store and pick up more formula as well as diapers, bottles, and other supplies. It was a good thing he went, because two hours later Jay was ready for his second feeding, right on schedule. I prepared another bottle just as before, fed him, and put him back in his crib.

I barely had time to get comfortable before he was crying for more. That baby sure could eat—it seemed that no more than an hour after finishing a bottle, he'd be hungry again. I was glad Phillip had bought a case of formula, because that child was going through it faster than I'd gone through pancakes, peanut butter, and watermelon when I was pregnant.

The thing was, Jay didn't seem to be putting on any weight. It didn't make sense: How could a baby eat so much and still look so scrawny? I thought the formula would last us a month, but he was less than a week old, and we were on our last can. So I asked Phillip to run out to the market and get some more. "What's it called again?" he said.

I picked up the last can, looked at the label, and my heart lurched.

"Oh, my gosh. Oh, my gosh," I said.

"What's the matter?" he said.

"Oh, Phillip, I can't believe what I've been doing! I've been mixing the formula with water, only it says right here, 'Do not dilute!' The nurse told me the hospital formula was concentrated and had to be diluted. But this kind was already diluted before they put it in the can."

I'd been starving my baby. My precious, firstborn son was a hungry, puny thing because I'd been feeding him watery formula for four days. I felt so horrible, so guilty, and so ridiculous.

Phillip went out for more formula. I must have examined that label fifty times before I fed that formula to Jay—and this time, I got it right. And he finally began putting on weight—until two weeks later, when he developed a digestive disorder and had to be rushed into surgery. But I'm getting ahead of myself.

The point is, as much as I don't want to admit it (we never do, do we?), there are a few things I wish I'd done differently. And even though I still cringe when I think about my early attempts to feed my baby, at the time I really was doing my best.

It's always been important for me to know I was doing the best I could at the time I was doing it, even if my best sometimes wasn't all that good. Both Jay and Jordan managed to survive my many mothering mishaps, which is a relief to me. I firmly believe that how happy my sons are is a reflection of who I am and how well I did my job. Being a mother is more than a phase in my life; for me, it's a never-ending mission, my calling here on earth. And when the time comes and I'm standing before my heavenly Father, I just want Him to say to me, "Job well done."

> Being a mother is more than a phase in my life; for me, it's a never-ending mission, my calling here on earth. And when the time comes and I'm standing before my heavenly Father, I just want Him to say to me, "Job well done."

You can look after your children every day, make sure they have clean clothes, and make sure they're at home every night, but there's more to mothering than that. I always wanted my boys to have joy inside of them, that peace and excitement and pride about who they are. I wanted to not only make sure they were physically taken care of but spiritually and emotionally taken care of, too. There are so many responsibilities to parenting, and I always wanted to make

sure I'd done everything I could to give them not only the basics they needed to stay alive, but the spirit and enthusiasm to really *be* alive, to live with passion and gusto and joy.

No one's perfect. My kids aren't perfect and I'm not perfect. We don't agree about everything, and every once in a while one of them will do something that makes me want to ask what in the heck they were thinking. But I can honestly say that I feel confident that I've done everything I'm capable of doing.

My goal from the moment our sons were born was not to raise them to be terrific two-year-olds and fabulous first-graders; it was to raise them to be effective, autonomous adults. Phillip often says on the show that parents aren't raising kids, they're raising adults, and I like to think that maybe he got that from me. Because from the day Jay and Jordan were born, I've always believed that my job was to prepare them for that faraway day when they would be on their own.

Now, with Jay working and Jordan in college, that faraway day has come. And let me tell you, that day came *fast*. When they were babies, people would always tell me to enjoy them while they were little, that before I knew it they'd be all grown up and I wouldn't know where the time had gone. And although I believed them, I didn't fully appreciate how quickly my boys would wiggle through my fingers like they used to in the bathtub and turn into the men they've become. If you have a son, you know what I mean: one day he's soft and tender and wrapping his arms around your waist; the next day he hugs you and your nose mashes up against his collarbone. You hug him back and feel how strong he has become, and how much bigger he is than you, and you think, *Oh my, this isn't a boy, this is a man—my little boy, my son, is a man.*

And in that moment, you can start sobbing—or you can stand up tall, unmash your nose, and get on with your life.

It's all about choice. When my boys were about to leave for college, I had a choice and I thought, *This is their time and I want them excited about it. If I sit around and cry and say, "Oh, I'm going to miss you, I don't want you to go,"* that would mean I was making their leaving all about me, and it's not about me; it's about them. I would have felt very selfish if I'd expressed my love by telling them, "Once you leave, I am going to get up every day and cry." What a burden to put on them! They've earned the right to go on and live this new phase in life. It was always important for my sons to know that I was there for them and that I am still here for them. I made a conscious choice to convince them that I was thrilled for them and that I knew they were going to do well.

And that's why, if I cried about them leaving, it was always in bed at night or in the bathtub (I give myself permission to cry day or night in the bathtub, because it's one my favorite places to be). My tears were for the joy of being their mother. And of course that came to an end, that daily mothering, when they left for college. But what did not come to an end was the joy I felt—and continue to feel—at being their mother. And that's because I made that conscious choice to celebrate their independence rather than grieve their absence. I chose, and continue to choose, to rejoice in their competence rather than mourn the fact that they don't need me anymore. Because, in fact, they do still need me, only in different ways than they used to. Just as they have grown and evolved, so have I; and just as they are excited about entering this new phase of their lives, so am I excited about entering this new phase in my life.

It's not that I don't miss them; I do. But it's all a matter of how you look at it: When our kids leave the nest, we can either mourn their departure as the end of a profoundly meaningful era in our lives, or embrace it as the beginning of a new one. We can either reject our children's coming of age and pretend they're still little kids who can't live without us, or we can accept that they've grown into the adults we hoped they'd become and get on with our lives.

I choose acceptance.

It's hard to overestimate the value of acceptance. Being able to accept what life dishes out is tremendously helpful. That's another choice I made: to love and accept Phillip as he was, and is, and will be. And boy, have I been tested on that one! After thirty years of marriage, I've had many, many opportunities to learn and grow in the acceptance department. And I've made remarkable progress, considering that I've not always had that accepting spirit.

That is not the same thing as having a loving spirit, which is something I've always had. Phillip knows exactly how I feel about him. I'm crazy about that man, and I tell him so almost every day. I think he is brilliant and wise, and a wonderful father and husband. He is the perfect man for me, and I cannot imagine being married to anyone else.

But that doesn't mean we're alike. In fact, we're quite different, and I confess that even after all these years together, I still don't understand him sometimes. For instance, there's Phillip's opinion of chocolate: to him, it's just another snack—like beer nuts or a piece of fruit. Now, I've got a huge bowl of fruit sitting on my kitchen counter, and I like a crisp apple or a juicy orange as much as the next girl. But to think of a melt-in-your-mouth bittersweet truffle as no different from a beer nut? I just don't get it.

Nor do I get his footwear philosophy. If you could see my closet, you'd understand: I must have a hundred pairs of shoes, and I can still find room for more. And girls, I know you know what I mean. A woman can never have too many shoes. But Phillip, he thinks three pairs of shoes is one pair too many.

And then there's the way he deals with news. When it comes to work, he's the most thorough guy in the world. But when it comes to personal matters, he never asks the right questions. He'll come home after work and say, "Oh, guess what? Joe and Elizabeth had their baby today." I'll get all excited and start asking questions.

"Oh my gosh, what'd they have?"

"I don't know," he'll say.

"You didn't ask?"

"No."

"Well, okay," I'll say, pressing on. "What did they name it?'"

"I don't know."

"Well then, how's Elizabeth doing?"

"I'm sure she's exhausted, Robin. She just had a baby."

Now, you ask a woman about some couple's blessed event, and she'll tell you the baby's name, how much it weighed, how long it was, how long the labor was, how many pushes it took to squeeze it out, and whether or not they're planning on having another one—and that's just for starters. But when it comes to women and what's important to them, men just don't ask the right questions.

I found that out the hard way. It happened more than twenty-three years ago, but the memory is as clear as day. It was a Saturday, and I was in the kitchen fixing dinner. Phillip had been out in the garage for about three hours, trying to find the source of a rattling noise in his car. So he comes in, sees I'm in the middle of cooking, and says, "Hey, can you shut this down for a little bit and come out and help me?"

Being the agreeable young wife I was trying to be back then, I said, "Sure, absolutely." I turned off the flame under the skillet and went out to the garage.

The first thing I noticed was my beautiful bath towel lying on the floor behind the car. It wasn't one of those old, raggedy towels you stack in the garage to wash your car. No, this was a cream colored, 100 percent Egyptian cotton towel with a big, beautiful *M* monogrammed in blue, one of those thirsty-type towels that's just perfect for drinking up all that oil and grease on the garage floor.

I stood there staring at the towel, and Phillip said, "I've been out here all afternoon and I can't find where that noise is coming from. And I'm just wondering if, you know, you would lie down on the towel and let me back the car out over you, and maybe you can hear the rattle from underneath."

I looked at the towel, I looked at the car, and I looked at him. And I said, "You know what? The only rattle I hear is the one in your head if you think I'm lying down on that towel."

"Oh, don't worry," he said. "You'll fit. I measured."

I just stood there and said, "No way, buddy. I am not getting under that car."

So he tried a different approach.

"Well, then," he said, "will you get in the car and help me?"

"Yes, I sure will," I said. "I can do that." So he opened the trunk and put the towel in there.

Well, ladies, I am embarrassed and ashamed to admit this, but I got in that trunk. I did. I got in and lay down on my beautiful towel, and Phillip lowered the lid a bit and showed me a cutout on the inside.

"Here's where you can hold the lid with your hand, and it won't close on you," he said. "I'm just going to back out a little, and you listen and see if you can tell where the noise is coming from."

I'm thinking we're going to run a few feet back and forth in the garage. Phillip starts the engine, backs out into the driveway, enters the cul-de-sac, and starts zooming around in circles—with me hanging on for dear life. He hits a bump, I close the lid on myself, I'm locked in the trunk, and he's still driving in circles. Now I'm screaming, "Phillip, stop the car! Stop the car!"

Finally the car stops. I hear him come around to the trunk but then he has to go back for his keys so he can open the lid. I hear the key in the lock, right near my head, and as the lid springs open, there's my husband with a hopeful look on his face.

Now, I'm going to tell you what he did not say.

He did not say, "Honey, what's wrong?"

Not, "Sweetheart, why are you crying?"

He did not say, "Oh, you're bleeding."

He didn't even say, "Oh here, baby, let me help you out."

No, my beloved husband lifted the trunk lid, gazed into my eyes and said, "Did you hear anything?"

Let's just say that I didn't hear anything, but he sure did. "How could you ask me to do that? What were you thinking? Didn't you notice the trunk was closed? Didn't you hear me screaming?" He just stared at me as if I were overreacting in a major way. To this day, he does not think it is odd that he asked me to do this.

The truth is, Phillip and I spent years being frustrated with each other, doing exactly what God intended each of us to do. He did not intend Phillip to be like me, and He did not intend me to be like Phillip. You wouldn't want to be married to someone like you anyway, would you? Would you really want to be married to someone who thinks like you, acts like you, and talks like you? I wouldn't, that's for sure. If Phillip did everything I wanted him to, he just wouldn't be him, and I wouldn't like that.

The man who put me in the trunk of his car is the same man who, when I was at my very lowest after losing both my parents, looked me in the eye and said, "I will never leave you. You are not alone."

And he was the same man who, for our twentieth wedding anniversary, gave me the most wonderful gift I have ever received. We had gone to dinner that night and were going to celebrate by spending the night in a beautiful hotel in Dallas. When we got up to the room, he handed me a gift.

It was a book bound in beautiful black leather, and written on the front, in silver embossed letters, was "Twenty-Year Spin." I opened it, and inside were twenty poems that Phillip had written. Each poem reflected a year of our marriage, from August 14, 1976, to that very day, August 14, 1996. Facing each poem was a collage of photographs depicting the major events of that year, starting with snapshots of our wedding showing Phillip in his white tuxedo and me in my wedding dress, and ending with a poem honoring our twentieth year: "If life were a garden and I could walk through again, you're the flower I would pick for another twenty-year spin."

> Accept him for the man he is, and accept yourself for the woman you are. Do not apologize for your feminine ways. God made you that way on purpose, and don't let anybody tell you there is anything wrong with being a woman and doing things as a woman does them.

I sat there for what felt like hours, savoring every poem, crying and wondering how he managed to remember so many events from so long ago. I remember asking him, "When did you write this? And when did you get these pictures? I never thought you even knew where I kept the photo albums!" And he told me he had written the poems mostly while he was either waiting in airports or waiting for court to come back into session (at the time, he was working for Courtroom Sciences, a litigation consulting firm he had founded).

I'll never forget how I felt when I opened that book. I didn't realize he had it in him to write one poem, let alone twenty. Never in a million years would I have imagined he'd do such a thing. After twenty years, he could still surprise me; and now, after thirty years, he is surprising me still.

Men are complex creatures whose ways seem just as mysterious to us as ours do to them. It isn't fair to accuse them of being unromantic or unloving just because their ways of creating romance and expressing love may be different from ours. My point is, don't expect your husband to be like you. Accept him for the man he is, and accept yourself for the woman you are. Do not apologize for your feminine ways. God made you that way on purpose, and don't let anybody tell you there is anything wrong with being a woman and doing things as a woman does them. Women need to be who they are and inspire their husbands to appreciate them *as they are.* I've always believed that women and men are fundamentally different, that being a feminine woman is just as powerful as being a manly man; and that's something I wish every woman would think about. If your husband makes fun of your feminine ways, tell him to try living without them for a while.

It's always been important for the men in my life to see and respect every side of me, to see my femininity and my strength, and to see that my femininity *is* my strength. When a man and woman are together, the man needs to feel that he's the stronger one in the room, and I don't have a problem with that. Men were put on this earth to stand in the doorway and protect their women and children, and I say, God bless them. I always make sure Phillip knows that I rely on his strength, and that I would miss him terribly if he weren't there. Which doesn't mean I'm not plenty strong in my own right: I am. It's just that I don't feel a need to compete with him for dominance in our relationship.

I've always seen a wonderful, supportive side of men that some women may not see. I think a lot of that has to do with the fact that I have a twin brother, and I showed Roger early on that he didn't always have to be the strongest just because he was the only boy in the family, that he could be vulnerable and I would always be there. I loved telling him, "Don't worry, I'll always be there for you and I'll always take care of you," when we were really young.

I think that's when my real love of mothering started, because I always wanted to take care of Roger, whether he wanted me to or not. We moved around a lot when I was a kid, and we were always transferring to different schools. I remember being in first grade and starting at a new school, and the teacher wanted Roger and me to stay late one day so she could test our reading skills and know where to place us in reading class.

She sat down with Roger at the desk in front of me, and told him he would be reading first. So Roger starts reading aloud, "See Spot run." But before he could get to the third word, I was saying it for him. He'd say, "See Spot—" and I'd say, "Run." He'd say, "Jane goes outside—" and I'd chime in, "To play."

After about ten minutes, the teacher said, "Robin honey, you're going to have to let him read his own words." And I was thinking, *Uh-oh, this is not good; she's not going to let me help him.* Not that he needed my help, mind you; Roger could read just as well as I could. I just felt an irresistible urge to protect him.

The teacher could see that I was like a little mother hen with him, so the next day she seated him in the first chair of the first row and put me in the last chair of the last row so I couldn't help him.

And—I'll never forget this—she said, "All right, children, we're going to learn to spell our names and write them down on the top of the paper."

And I'm thinking, *Jameson . . . Can Roger spell "Jameson"?* So I stared at Roger and he turned around and looked at me and I whispered, "J," hissing it up the row so he could hear me. He turned around and wrote it down and spun around again and I hissed, "A," and it went on like that until I had spelled out our last name for him. And I thought, *Okay, this will work out fine.*

Or so I thought until the phone rang that night. It was my teacher, and my mother got on and after a while I heard her saying, "Separate them? Oh, I don't know, that's not going to be good . . . You can't separate them, they have to be together." It was clear to me as I stood there eavesdropping that the teacher was saying I was helping Roger too much and had to be put in a different class. My mother listened for a while and then said, "All right, but if you do separate them, you're going to have to put him in a room where she can look in and see him and make sure he's okay."

That was my mother for you, doing the right thing for our education but also making sure our needs were considered. And sure enough, the next day they moved Roger to the classroom across the hall, and moved my seat up from the back row to a spot right in front of the doorway where I could look up every few minutes and see that he was okay. I looked across that hall every ten minutes, and waited until he looked at me so I could tell from his face that he was okay.

So I've always seen the vulnerable side of men: They are very open, they want to be happy, they want to be loved, and they want to get along. They can also be tender and unexpectedly defenseless, and sometimes need to turn to their women for strength. If you give a man a safe haven to show his soft and gentle side, and let him know you still think he's strong, I think it makes for a perfect relationship.

You've got to get beneath the surface to know who a man really is. From the day I met Phillip, I knew he was a dear, loving person. But to this day, when I introduce him to people, a lot of times they say, "Ooh, your husband scares me." And I've got to admit I had a similar reaction for the first few minutes when I met him thirty-five years ago but I quickly saw that he's the most adorable man ever.

> I have chosen to bring a spirit of acceptance to my relationship with Phillip, and to embrace the differences between us rather than resist them.

But because of the way I grew up, I've always looked past what a lot of men put out there, and chosen to see them as large-scale boys who just want to be loved. And when you do that, it's not hard at all to make them happy.

And what makes them happy is to be accepted. That is why I have chosen to bring a spirit of acceptance to my relationship with Phillip, and to embrace the differences between us rather than resist them. And that is why I don't think we should judge our husbands too harshly. We have to accept our mates' ways because that's what makes life interesting.

I'll be coming back to this acceptance idea throughout the book, because it's such an important part of what makes our marriage work. I know now that just because Phillip loves me, doesn't mean he's supposed to think the way I do, or act the way I do, or know you're not supposed to put a thirty-five-dollar bath towel on the garage floor (or your wife in the trunk of your car). I know now that a big part of marriage is not wishing my husband were more like me, but accepting and actually enjoying the fact that he isn't.

On the other hand, I have also learned that just because I have chosen to be half of a couple, doesn't mean I have to stop being who God designed me to be: a loving, amiable wife who is her own person, thinks for herself, and knows that there's more to a working marriage than maintaining a monogrammed towel in pristine condition. After all, Phillip thought he was doing the right thing; he did give me a nice clean, thick towel to lie down on.

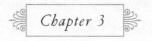

Chapter 3

A DAUGHTER'S HEART
Choosing My Own Legacy

If I had to name one consistent thing about me, it's that I've always been focused and very much in control of those parts of my life that can be controlled or influenced. We cannot choose our genetics; our sex, how tall we'll be, and our race are all decided by our DNA. But at the same, a great deal of our experience in this world *is* up to us, and I never wanted to leave the aspects I could control in anyone else's hands.

From an early age, I had absolutely no idea who, if anyone, I could count on to pursue that which was in my best interests; to pursue what I wanted and needed, what encouraged and protected my dreams. When you never know where you will live tomorrow or if there will be enough food to eat, you learn to look within to find a way to survive and to thrive.

My mother was the sweetest, gentlest woman you could ever meet. I remember her always saying that it was a privilege to be our mother. That was her spirit: she loved being a mother, and I know I get that from her. Georgia Mae Drake Jameson always put her family first, and did her best to provide us with clean clothes, three meals a day, and all the love we could stand. But even her best efforts could not tame the chaos of being married to an alcoholic. As a result, I grew up surrounded by uncertainty. Ironically, the source of much of that uncertainty was also the person whose ferocious love played a huge part in defining both who I was and who I am, and that person was my father, Jim Jameson.

My father absolutely adored me, and I adored him. He was the most loving, giving, protective person, the best man in the world. He loved all five of us kids and made each of us feel as if we might just be his favorite. So I woke up every day feeling very, very loved.

He was also crazy about my mother. She was about five foot four with beautiful blue eyes and very dark hair that she wore short and stylish. She had the most beautiful legs and was kind of plump (after five kids, who can blame her?), but on her it looked good. She was a womanly woman, and she smiled all the time.

For all his flaws, my father was a hard worker. He managed a car dealership Monday through Friday and moved from lot to lot as I was growing up. My parents always drove brand-new cars, demonstrator models they had on the lot to show off the auto-maker's latest line. My parents never owned these cars, but they were new and spiffy, and we kids always felt proud of that.

My father also bought a small driving range, where people

could hit golf balls, as a side business. Someone ran it for him during the week, and my dad would work there on weekends. We were often with him; my sisters, Roger, and I worked there during the summer and after school. We would have to go every Saturday and Sunday afternoon to pick up golf balls—thousands of golf balls. I don't remember minding too much, because we all knew if we didn't help out, my father would have to pay someone else to do the work, and we couldn't afford it. The twenty dollars he would have had to pay someone else to gather the balls was often the difference between having groceries and not having them.

Of course, the reason we couldn't afford it was that my father squandered the bulk of his earnings on drinking and gambling, and there wasn't much left for the family. But this was never discussed; we all pitched in because this was just the way life was. We didn't feel deprived or needy because my father didn't tell us he had lost two weeks' earnings on his last binge, and my mother didn't mention it, either. They just told us we had to help out at the driving range that weekend, and we went.

That said, we weren't completely unaware of the situation; the fact that I never had store-bought clothes until after high school wasn't lost on me. As I mentioned earlier, my mother made all my clothes—that is, the ones that weren't handed down from my sisters. Jamie was born seven years before I was, then came Cindi two years later, and Karin two years after that. By the time Roger and I were born in 1953, my mother had a closet full of "vintage" girls' clothes just waiting for me to grow into. Roger was lucky; he got all new clothes to wear because he was the only boy.

My mother was an amazing seamstress. But one thing she couldn't make was jeans, and for a high-school girl back in the early seventies, this was a problem. I remember once asking my father if we could afford ten or fifteen dollars—it wasn't any more than that—for me to go buy a pair of jeans. He gazed at me with this sad look on his face. He wanted to give it to me, but he just didn't have it. So, yes, I dreamed of the day when I could afford to buy new clothes (and believe me, I've made good on that dream). But for the most part, I wore what my mother sewed for me.

She started out using an old-fashioned sewing machine, the kind with a treadle you pushed with your feet, and I remember what a big deal it was when she got an electric machine. Sewing was a creative outlet for her. She loved going to fabric stores, and she'd come home with armloads of remnants and patterns and trim and lay it all out so she could see what she had to work with. She seldom bought the fabric she wanted because it was too expensive so instead she bought what was left over and stockpiled it. She had towers of fabric stacked up against her bedroom wall because she was planning to make something with it one day. I remember my father making snide remarks about her fabric addiction, and I also remember thinking, *Well, look who's talking—at least her addiction keeps her home at night.* (I didn't say it, but I thought it.)

What strikes me about my childhood is the sense of feeling both very much loved and very uncertain at the same time. I'm sure that's what made me so intent on being in control of my life. It's not unusual for children of alcoholics to grow into adults who require a high degree of control, because they had so little of it when they were children. But what makes my story different from many others I've heard is that as much as my father's drinking hurt me, I still think of him with great love and devotion.

It must be over forty years ago, but I always go back to this one day when I think about my father. I was doing some kind of play or performance at school and he was coming. I was very excited and I ran and knocked on his bedroom door and said, "daddy, wear your red sweater today."

He said, "Okay, darling"—he always called me darling—"Okay, darling, I will." I always go to that memory of opening his bedroom door and looking in there and seeing him light up when I entered the room. He thought I was funny, and I made him laugh. In return, he made me feel as if I mattered, as if me wanting him to wear his red sweater was enough of a reason for him to wear it. I always felt happy and loved when I was with my father. It didn't matter what we were doing. I just wanted to be connected with him, to be with him all the time. And after he died, I took that sweater, folded it in tissue paper, and kept it in my closet so on those days when I missed him most, I could hold it against my face and remember how special he made me feel.

I can remember only one time that he was annoyed with me. I was probably five or six at the time, and he had asked me to go out onto the front porch and help him change a light bulb. Now, back then, I was always moving and squirming; I never sat still. At the dinner table, he'd say, "Robin, you're going to have to sit still now, darling, so we can have dinner." I was horsing around once and got my finger wedged in between a couple of slats on the chair, and I was sitting there with my arm bent back behind me. And he said, "Robin, darling, you're going to have to sit still now and put your hands in your lap." And I said, "I can't, daddy, because my finger is caught in the back of the chair." And he started laughing so hard I thought he'd have to leave the table.

So on this occasion we went out to the porch and he said, "Do you think you can stand still long enough to hold this new light bulb while I take out the old one?" And I said, "Sure I can, daddy." And of course, I dropped the light bulb and it shattered, and little pieces of glass flew all over the place.

Oh, my gosh . . . the look on his face.

That was the only time in my entire life that I can remember my father being upset with me. He just glared and said, "Oh! I cannot believe you did that! I asked you—can you not be still? We don't have another light bulb. What are we supposed to do now?" And when I think about it, I realize it was an important moment in my life. Because as annoyed as he was with me, I just knew he wouldn't stay that way very long.

And he didn't, of course; within five minutes, I was back in his arms and all was forgiven, because all I had to do was say, "Oh, I'm sorry, daddy," and his heart would melt. I knew he'd get over it because he was just too crazy about me not to. That was the good part of my father.

There was another part, too, a part that had to do with him drinking and not coming home and us not knowing where he was, whom he was with, or what he was doing. It didn't seem to go with the rest of him, and yet there it was. And the thing that made it feel so out of control was that we never saw that part of him. What we did see was the fallout from his drunkenness, and how it affected my mother. And every once in a while, we got to see my mother for the hero that she was.

One such episode is forever alive in my memory. It was probably three o'clock in the morning when the commotion began. I was fourteen and groggy with sleep, but the banging startled me awake and dragged me from my bed and toward the front hallway.

My room was in the rear of the house, so the pounding wasn't as loud for me as it was for my mother, whose bedroom was just to the left of the front door. That's where I found her, tense and braced for battle, her right hand on the round brass knob and her left on the chain, making sure it was secure.

"You stay back there," she said, jutting her chin toward the kitchen behind me. "I'll handle this." I wanted to be up there with her but I knew better; when my mother told you to get back, you got back. I opened my mouth to call to my brother, whose bedroom was ahead and just off to the side, but changed my mind. Roger was a heavy sleeper and I didn't want to cry out because if I did, whoever was on the other side of that door would know we were there, waiting for him to come and get us.

My father wasn't home. None of us had seen him since he left to play golf two days earlier. He would do that a lot when we were kids, get up early on Sunday, announce he was heading out to the driving range and then on to the golf course, and walk out to the car with his golf bag slung over his shoulder. My mother and the rest of us would spend the day without him, glancing out the window whenever a Chevy swung by that sounded like his. All the time I was growing up, he'd head out to work and then to the club on Sunday and we wouldn't know if he'd be back for lunch, or dinner, or at all that night. We'd eat supper without him, and clean up the kitchen and watch the *Ed Sullivan Show* without him, and I'd go to bed hoping he would come home for my mother's sake, if not for mine. I would wake myself up an hour later to see if maybe he had just played cards somewhere and come home late; I would glide silently to my parents' bedroom, peek inside, and see my mother reading a magazine or ironing one of his shirts and I'd know he wasn't there. The next morning I would ask my mother if daddy was home, and she would say, "No, he is not," not quite looking at me, and then we wouldn't talk about it. I would turn away and finish my breakfast and leave for school and life would go on with my father gone. And he would stay gone.

All this raced through my mind as I stood in the hallway in my pajamas, waiting to see what my mother would do. The door shuddered again as something hard—a fist, maybe, or a beer can or a bat—pounded it, along with the raucous bellowing of men. I knew my father was on a binge because he hadn't been home in two days; there was no way he was going to show up and rescue us.

My mother cinched the belt of her bathrobe and I saw something in her back that spoke more of fight than of fear. I retreated to the kitchen doorway and watched as she turned the knob, pulled the door open, and looked through the opening for what felt like forever.

"Who are you? What do you want?" Her voice had an edge to it, sharp and clear.

"We've come for our things." The voice was deep and slurred. He might be big, and he was definitely drunk. "We've come for our things and we're not leaving without them." I leaned to the left and peered outside. In the slice of darkness between the door and its wooden frame, I could make out several pairs of legs and dangling shirttails; my mother's head obscured the rest.

"Your things?" my mother said. "What are you talking about?" A set of legs moved closer to the door as my mother braced it with her leg.

"I'm talking about the things that's ours, what we won."

"What you won? What are you talking about? Where's Jim?"

"Jim's who sent us. He anted up your furniture in a game of five-card stud, and he lost, and we're not leaving without it." The man stepped back. He was the biggest of the lot; one of the other two was downright stringy, and none of them looked too steady on their feet. But there were three of them, and the big one had boots on. If he kicked the door, the chain would snap and they'd be inside. Now the skinny one sidled over.

"Look, lady," he said. "We won the stuff fair and square. It's Jim who wagered it and him that sent us, so just get out of the way and let us get what's ours."

I was thunderstruck. My father—my sweet, loving father who adored and cared for me—my father wasn't going to save me from these men, my father *knew* these men: knew them, sat at a table with them, drank with them, dealt cards with them, and gambled away our furniture to them in a poker game. My dear, sweet father had given these men our address, sent them to our house, and left my mother to fight them off in a beige chenille bathrobe while they tried to take the bed I'd been sleeping in since I was three.

It was one of those moments you remember forever, a dazzling dose of clarity that obliterates your childhood and rams you into the realm of real life. It sends a shiver through your soul because— for the first time—you are bearing witness to the truth. If I had been teetering on the brink of womanhood, this moment pushed me over the edge, because it was then that it came to me that my daddy was a drunk.

You see, my father was not a mean drunk, as they call it; in fact, for years and years, we never saw him drunk at all. He was the type of alcoholic who would stay away when he was drinking and come home stone-cold sober. We never saw him loose or sloppy, loud or ornery; we just knew he drank, and that he did it away from us. As we got older and stayed up later, he would come home sometimes when we were awake. I think I was in middle school when I saw him drunk for the first time; then when he came home, he was funny. He would amuse us by telling us stories about the golf course, or showing us, very slowly and very deliberately, how he had set the ball on the tee just so, and swung his club just so, and then smacked the ball into a pond or a sand trap. He was just tipsy enough to look ridiculous as he pantomimed setting up the shot, and he was sweet and goofy and funny and he made us laugh.

But these men were not funny; they were loud and belligerent and growling that they wanted what was coming to them, all the while edging closer to that flimsy little chain. There was no screen door, no storm door, just the old wooden door I'd pushed open a thousand times without ever realizing how rickety it was. I was up close behind my mother now along with Roger, who had emerged from his bedroom wild-eyed in his pajamas and wondering what the heck was going on. We cowered there behind her, a five-foot four-inch column of chenille with an attitude.

"Now you listen," she said. "You're not coming into my house. I don't care what right you think you have but you are not coming into my house. You want your things? Fine—have your wives call me in the morning and we'll arrange it. You tell your wives to call me, and I'll talk to them about getting you your things." The word *things* came out somewhere between a snort and a snarl, in a tone of voice I'd never heard from her before. And she didn't move, just stared at them through that chink in the doorway, holding her ground. Then she shoved the door closed with her leg and her shoulder, reached for the wall switch and turned out the porch light, and turned to face my brother and me.

"Y'all go back to bed now," she said. "No one's coming in here, and nothing's going to happen." Her eyes were steady and her voice was steel. "Just go back to bed. Everything's going to be fine. I'll talk to the women in the morning. Not a stick of furniture is going to leave this house, you hear? Not a single knob from a single drawer. Nothing. Now go back to bed."

I remember crawling into bed with her, and her sobbing and me crying after a while. But as traumatic as that evening was, I fell asleep knowing that even if a hundred men had stood on that porch clamoring to come inside, my mother would never have let them in. As terrible and as scary as it was, I felt a real peace in knowing that no matter what slouched onto our doorstep, my mother wasn't going to let it in, and no matter what it threatened to do to us, my mother wasn't going to let it happen.

I learned a lot that night. Among other things, I learned that I would protect my children, my home, and my family with all my might, just as my mother had done. My mother was never going to allow anyone to invade the sanctuary that was our home and our lives. That was her domain, the three-bedroom, two-bath holy tract of her life's work, and she defended it with a fierceness that struck awe in my heart. She combined the instincts of a street fighter with the confidence of a queen, and showed me what real courage looked like.

When I picture that precious little woman standing at that door telling those brawling, nasty men, *You're not coming into my house. I don't care what right you think you have but you will not come into my house,* I still feel awed by the grace and dignity she mustered in the face of what felt to my fourteen-year-old self like the end of life as I had known it. What a brilliant woman! It was a move of sheer genius, invoking her inalienable right as a woman to remove herself from the crass company of those men and deal instead with their more refined helpmates. What were those guys going to do? What sort of brute would play poker with a man, beat his sorry rear end, and then interfere with his wife and mother of his children by forcing his way into her home?

When I told this story to Phillip's mother and sisters, they stared, wide-eyed and incredulous, when I described those rough-necks trying to boss my mother around. "What did she say? What did she *do*?" they all wanted to know. And when I told them she disarmed those guys by transforming it from a debt issue into a woman's issue, it had the same effect as the scene in *The Wizard of Oz* when Glinda the Good Witch told Dorothy she'd had the power to go home all along. My mother's womanly self-awareness was her ruby slippers: she knew she couldn't beat those men at their game, so she trashed the rules and created her own. It was one of the oldest strategies known to man, deployed by a woman ahead of her time. Even back then, my mother understood that sisterhood was far more powerful than a trio of drunken cowboys proving their manhood by carrying off a teenage girl's bedroom set. She knew that, in the sober light of morning, there weren't many wives who would conspire with their soused spouses to make off with another woman's furniture, poker game or not.

> My mother was never going to allow anyone to invade the sanctuary that was our home and our lives. That was her domain, the three-bedroom, two-bath holy tract of her life's work, and she defended it with a fierceness that struck awe in my heart.

The next morning we did not talk about it at all; that was how our family functioned ("dysfunctioned" would be more accurate). My mother smiled and asked Roger and me what we wanted for breakfast, not for a moment acting as if the Formica table we were eating on might be history by lunch. But then the phone rang and I could tell by the way my mother held the receiver with both hands that it was one of the wives calling. I was late for school but I stood in the kitchen, glued to the linoleum, watching as my mother wound herself up in the telephone cord and said, "That's all right, thank you, I knew you'd understand," over and over until I knew the woman was apologizing for what her husband had done and telling my mother there was no way she would take our furniture. And then my mother hung up the phone and started crying because she was talking to another woman, and the woman had understood. One of Phillip's life laws is that either you get it or you don't, and this woman got it. She said she didn't need our furniture, but even if she did need it, I can't imagine her hauling my mother's sofa out of our house and into hers because her husband and his buddies had had too many drinks and won a few rounds of poker off a guy who was even more hammered than they were.

Nor could I imagine at the time that that my father would drink, gamble, allow our furniture to be part of a card game, lose it, and not even have the decency to call my mother and say, "Oh, by the way, I'm completely soused, I've lost all our furniture, and these buddies of mine are coming to get it." He didn't even have the decency to prepare my mother for three drunken men to show up and pound on the door like thugs. I remember walking to school that morning wondering if when I came home, the living room and dining room and bedrooms would be empty, and we'd all have to sleep on the floor for the rest of our lives. Because as far as I knew, my mother had spoken to only one of those wives, and the other two might not be as merciful as the first. I never found out if the other two women called. But when we came home from school that day the furniture was still there, and we never lost it. Nor did we ever speak of that evening again.

It's forty years later but that memory is as fresh as a newly minted nightmare. It was one of those learning experiences that is so painful, you wonder if you'll survive. Then, when it's over, you look around at the wreckage of what used to be your world and you think to yourself: *This was hard, and I wish it hadn't happened. But it did, and I survived. Now, what have I learned from all this? How can I take this mess and use it to make things better for myself?*

What I learned was that life is complicated and love does not conquer all. I learned that as much as my father loved me, he wasn't strong enough to save me from his disease; and as much as I adored him, there were aspects of him that I disliked intensely. I learned that I admired my mother's fierceness that night, and that one day I would protect my own children as she had protected us. But I also learned that her refusal to acknowledge my father's alcoholism had backfired, and her strategy of pretending nothing was wrong was one that would not work for me.

> What I took away from the wreckage of that night was the knowledge that my parents were only human and therefore fallible, and to think as they did and duplicate their actions would be to live their lives and not my own.

What I took away from the wreckage of that night was the knowledge that my parents were only human and therefore fallible, and to think as they did and duplicate their actions would be to live their lives and not my own. I knew then that to live my own life, I would have to pick and choose among the many examples my parents had set for me, and decide which to emulate and which to discard. I didn't hate my parents for the life we lived, not even for the bad and scary parts. But I also knew I would never, ever allow those nightmares to be part of my own family's life. I knew with all my heart that my children would never have to stand behind a door while drunken men, sent by their own drunken father, pounded on it. I made the choice to embrace those parts of my parents' legacy that were good and wholesome, and to absolutely, categorically reject the rest.

In fact, that's what each of us has to do if we want to be truly autonomous, truly our own selves, and take our lives to the next level. And, contrary to the promises of our quick-fix culture, it doesn't happen overnight.

It took years for me to work through my feelings about my parents, especially my father. When I was a little girl, I derived a profound satisfaction from making my father laugh. I see now that what felt so good was that, for those few seconds when he smiled at me, I saw joy in his eyes, and I knew I had brought it to him. I knew that his drinking was a burden on both him and our family, but my mother always said it was an illness. And when he would climb up the front steps after three days away, clothes wrinkled and grimy and chin covered with stubble, my mother would avert her eyes and whisper, "He can't help it."

So I grew up thinking there was nothing my father could do

about this sickness he had, that it had a stranglehold on him, and if he could shake it, he would. I imagined it was like chicken pox or cancer, something that came over you, invaded you, that you simply had to endure. That's how I viewed all his destructive habits: he smoked, he drank, he gambled, but it was all due to this illness he had, the one he couldn't help. It didn't occur to me that he could take any action against it or weaken its power through an act of will.

It wasn't until I got older that I realized that he had at least some choice, that he had the ability to decide he was not going to let this disease control his life. At first it saddened me to realize he wasn't doing anything to fight his demons; then it pained me that he had allowed them to terrorize our lives. What I eventually came back to was that my father was not wholly a victim and that he bore some responsibility for abdicating control of his life. It was a stunning revelation, and it shaped the way I decided to live my own life. Today, I honor my father's memory by not letting anything control my life unless it's something I want in my life.

That's what I meant earlier when I talked about dedicating my life to undoing the legacy of doubt, fear, and pain that accompanied my father's great love for us. My father taught me how good it felt to be really loved, and I vowed that when I had children someday, they would also feel really loved. But I also vowed to raise my children without the terrible uncertainty I grew up with. I promised myself that any children I brought into this world would grow up not only feeling loved, but also feeling supported by a consistent level of certainty that I never had as a child.

I am happy to say I have kept that promise, and I kept it both by the grace of God and the gift of free will. I kept this promise to my children by vowing not to marry a man who drank or gambled. And the fact that my children's father doesn't drink or gamble isn't a matter of chance, it's a matter of choice. It's no accident that Phillip embodies the values I wanted for the father of my children; the only reason he's the father of my children is *because* he embodies those values, and did when we were dating. That's why I chose him, and that's why I wanted him to choose me. I am certain he had similar standards that I met as well.

I keep coming back to this issue of making choices because I know so many people who don't realize they have the right to choose how they live, people who would be so much happier if only they would examine the connection between what they do and how their lives turn out. They think their lives are predetermined, that things will always fall short of their expectations because that's just the way things go for them. They tell me that I'm different from them, that I'm so lucky, that I have the perfect life, the perfect marriage, perfect children, and the perfect house.

Well, guess what? Nothing is perfect. I'm not, my marriage isn't,

Phillip isn't, our kids aren't, and the house isn't (although there is one room that comes close). When it looks as if people have all this great stuff going on, it's only because it's right for *them,* and that's because they did their best to make it that way. As for being lucky, forget about it. It's not about luck; it's about figuring out what you want and making it happen. And it's about being honest, both with yourself and with the people who matter to you, when things aren't quite the way you want them to be. Sweeping unpleasantness under the rug and refusing to talk about it, as my mother did, is not a viable route to happiness.

That's one of the reasons our marriage works so well: we talk. We have always talked. We talked before we got married about what we expected from each other, and what we could and could not live with.

That's one of the reasons our marriage works so well: we talk. We have always talked. We talked before we got married about what we expected from each other, and what we could and could not live with. And while Phillip was more than happy to talk about these things, it was I who started the conversation. If this man was going to spend the rest of his life with me, I figured he should know what he was getting himself into.

I remember telling Phillip when I met him—his father was also an alcoholic, by the way—that there were both good things and bad things about my father, and that I was going to let go of the bad and embrace the good. I told him something my father often told my brother, "Women are to be respected; they are to be treated with dignity. We are the only two men in this house with five women, and it is our job to protect them, to look out for them, and to always treat them with respect. Do not use foul language around them and do not walk into the room without a shirt on. Adore these women and respect who they are." I heard my father say this all the time.

And I also told Phillip from almost day one: "You need to know right now: I cannot live with a man who drinks, and I cannot live with a man who gambles, and I will not live with a man who does not treat me with dignity, or respect who I am. I don't like foul language, and I cannot and will not ever put up with that. There are just certain things I cannot live with, and certain things I cannot live without." These words came directly out of growing up with two loving, human, flawed parents whose choices I identified as theirs and not my own.

Unlike my parents, who seldom (if ever) discussed the dynamics of their marriage, Phillip and I talked and negotiated for years about what we wanted in each other and how we wanted our marriage to be. We sat down and told each other, "Here's what I have to have, and here's what I will not tolerate." Phillip listened to me, and he has worked every day of our relationship—and I do mean every single day—to treat me the way I want and need to be treated. If you watch his show, you have probably heard him say that we teach people how to treat us, and you can be sure that I taught him exactly how to treat me. And he's been a superb student.

He is also an experienced teacher because, as it turned out, I also had a thing or two to learn.

When I was growing up and my father said something I didn't like, I pouted, and then I usually got what I wanted. I'd sulk and I wouldn't talk and I wouldn't look at him, and he just hated that, so sooner or later, I got my way. This worked well for me, and I stashed it in my collection of viable relationship techniques. Then, years later when I was dating Phillip, he said something once that I wasn't crazy about. I don't recall what it was, but I do recall that it bothered me, so I got all quiet and pensive; I probably even stuck out my lower lip. This went on for a while, maybe even a couple of days, before Phillip sat me down for a chat.

"You've got to know right now," he said, "that I can't put up with pouting. If I've done something, just tell me. Because when I ask you what's wrong and you say, 'Nothing,' and then I say, 'No really, it's obvious something is wrong; what are you upset about?' and you say, 'Nothing, nothing,' I've got to tell you—that doesn't work for me.

"Robin," he said, "if I ever do anything to upset you, I want you to promise me two things. Number one, that you will tell yourself that I did not do it on purpose, because I'm going to tell you right now: I will never, ever do anything to hurt you on purpose; if I do hurt you, it's just that I didn't know what I said or did would upset you. So promise me you'll tell yourself, 'He didn't really know it would upset me.' Number two, promise that you'll just come and tell me what I've done, because if you tell me what I did, I can tell you right now, I will never do it again."

That sounded good, so I said fine, and told him he should do the same with me. But I'd never had to do that before, and it took me awhile to muster the courage to tell him the truth. But I finally said, "Well, okay, fine. The other day you said something that really hurt my feelings." And he said, "Okay, I'm sorry. I won't say that anymore."

But what if he hadn't said that? What if he had told me to lighten up and learn to get over my hurt feelings? What if he had told me that he loved me but couldn't promise that he would never stay out all night drinking, or never place a bet on a horse?

I would have moved on, that's what. Oh, yes, I would.

As much as we love our men, the one thing we need to love even more is *ourselves*. Only we can know what we need to do to survive, to flourish, and harnessing ourselves to someone who brings chaos into our lives is not it. We are worthy; we are worth being loyal to; we are worth our men saying, "Yes, you are the most important person in my life."

As much as I wanted to marry Phillip, it wasn't about me holding on to him at any cost; it was about me holding on to me. I always wanted to be the most important part of my husband's life, whomever I married. If it wasn't going to be Phillip McGraw, it would be someone else. And whomever it was, no one and nothing would be more important to him than I was. My mother and father were crazy about each other, and I'd seen how good that was; the fact that my father was an alcoholic didn't change the way he felt about my mother. He thought she was the cutest, sweetest woman alive. I loved that about him, and I chose to bring that part of him into my life by deciding I would make my husband feel that way about me.

I brought a lot of my mother with me, too. My mother talked all the time (so do I), and she laughed at everything. We lived paycheck to paycheck, but she had the attitude that when her children were around, it was Christmas every day. She read cookbooks as if they were novels and on Sundays she read the food section in the newspaper. She was always trying new recipes. And I'm not talking frozen entrées; I'm talking home-style cooking from scratch that made the house smell of warmth and well-being and love. Meatloaf. Fried chicken. Stews.

She also loved to make desserts and was a terrific pastry chef. No matter how low on money we were, we always had a new dessert for a treat. It was one of the many ways she showed us that she loved us. My favorite was her red velvet cake. She made it from scratch, the cake and the frosting, and always on our birthdays we got to pick whatever kind of cake we wanted. And she did everything in this little walk-through kitchen with a four-burner gas stove, a chipped sink, and hardly any counter space at all. Whenever I hear someone say she'd cook dinner more often if only she had a better oven or more counter space (preferably the granite variety), I think of my mother smiling and rolling out pastry dough on her scratched-up Formica countertops. Then I have to smile, too.

But I never forget her steely side, because that's in me, too. The strength she mustered to keep those men out of our house that night is the same strength she used to keep the family together all those times when my father gambled away the rent and the grocery money. It's not an easy job to love a drinker, but her heart was in her work and she kept us safe and fed and warm whether my dad was around or not. She protected us, and she did her best to preserve the illusion that our household was just like any other, and that everything was fine.

Until one day years later when we were all grown and out of the house, and she looked at my father, announced, "That's it—I'm not going to live like this anymore," and filed for divorce.

Talk about shock and awe.

I was shocked, but so proud of her, so very proud. I felt sorry for my father because he loved my mother and needed her so much, and I knew he'd be devastated. But she took a stand, said she wasn't going to live one more day with an alcoholic, and laid down the law. I remember her telling me, "Robin, I love your father, but I have a right to live without alcoholism. And if this is what it takes to make him stop drinking, then I'm going to do it." It wasn't so much that she was leaving him as she was refusing to live with his addiction. She left the door open so if he stopped drinking, she could come back. You could say that she really did it for both of them, but the bottom line was, she did it. She filed the papers, packed a suitcase, and left town to go stay with my sister for a while.

She had been gone about a week when my phone rang. I was in my midtwenties and had been married for a few years and was living not far from my parents. It was my father on the phone, and I could tell from the sound of his voice that he was trying to come down off a drinking binge. He told me he was at home, and asked if I could please bring him something to eat.

I remember staring at the curly cord that connected the phone to the receiver that I held to my ear, as if trying to focus on something solid and real while the last illusion of my childhood faded away. He had never made me face the truth before. It was as if he had said, "Robin, darling, you're going to have to sit still now so we can have dinner, except I'm too drunk to do anything for myself and I need you to bring dinner to me."

My mother had always been the one to help him, serve him a meal, clean up after him, and help him get sober. But she was staying with my sister, and it was probably the first time he had ever tried to sober up on his own. He sounded so weak and pitiful, and I felt sorry for him and frustrated with him at the same time. Here he was, having driven my mother away because he couldn't stay away from the bottle all those years, and he still didn't have the gumption to take control of his life. But then my heart began to ache as I realized how hard it must have been for him to call me, his adoring daughter who used to look up to him, and acknowledge that he was too wasted to take care of himself.

I didn't know what to feel. I was disappointed that he was too weak to get sober and win my mother back, and ticked off that he seemed to care more for whisky than he did for her. And I was resentful that he was substituting me for my mother, expecting me to become his caretaker when he was too irresponsible to take care of himself. But then the anger abated and I imagined him rattling around the house all by himself, defeated and alone, and my heart broke. This poor, pathetic, aging man was my beloved father, the charming, youthful man whose enduring, relentless affection made me feel beautiful and loved throughout my life. How could I turn away from him?

I looked at Phillip and he saw the confusion in my eyes. He said,

"Robin, you need to do this for him. This is not the time to take a stand; we don't want him starving to death." So I fixed him a plate of his favorite food, took it over on a tray, set it outside the front door, rang the doorbell, and left. I had enough compassion to not want him to have to face me drunk, and enough respect for myself to not have to see him that way.

Eventually, my father enrolled in Alcoholics Anonymous so my mother would come back to him. Once he got sober and convinced her he would stay sober, she withdrew her petition for divorce. My mother lived for only six years after she returned to my father, but it brings me a real peace to know she lived the last years of her life happily with him because he never drank again.

> It doesn't matter how loving, how kind, or how good you are; when alcoholism is controlling your life, goodness, kindness, and love don't help.

As I write these words and relive those days, I am tempted to imagine what things might be like had I repeated the patterns of my parents' lives. But when I try to picture Jordan or Jay having to come over here to take care of their drunken mother, the scene goes dark because it's too preposterous for me to visualize. I cannot picture it because I won't allow it; it will never happen, end of story.

That is my legacy to my children: I am not going to live like that, and I am not going to make them live like that. It doesn't matter how loving, how kind, or how good you are; when alcoholism is controlling your life, goodness, kindness, and love don't help.

There comes a time when you have to look deep within yourself and say, *As good a person as I am, as kind as I am, as loving as I am, that's still not enough. I have to respect myself and do what it takes to be able to live my life in a way that makes me proud.* As women, it is our responsibility to respect ourselves and do what it takes to live our lives in ways that make us proud. We need to live this truth every day.

Chapter 4

A Heart of Clarity and Conviction

Choosing to Go After What I Want

Knowing what you want will get you only so far; the next step is getting it. And judging from my observations of human nature over the last half-century, it's the getting, not the wanting, that gives people trouble.

Especially women. Lord, I don't know what it is with us, but we sure seem to settle for less than we ought to. Considering that we are acknowledged to be the more intuitive half of the human race, we don't do much to press our advantage. How many men do you know who pick up on the subtleties of human behavior the way women do? It has nothing to do with intelligence and everything to do with the unique way women perceive things.

It's happened more than once that Phillip and I have been out to dinner with another couple, and something about the way they're looking at each other tells me that something's up with them. In the car going home I'll say, "Phillip, did you notice how they were acting tonight?" And he'll look at me as if I'm from another planet and say, no, he didn't notice anything at all. And then a few days later I run into that woman and she says she's sorry if she and her husband seemed weird that night, but they'd had this little disagreement before they left the house. And I'll go home, and, in a blaze of triumph, tell Phillip what she said; and he'll just look at me as if to say, "And your point is?"

My point is that women are born with gifts of discernment that we could, and should, use to get what we want out of life. But too many of us decline to use our gifts, accepting what comes our way rather than taking charge and making sure that what comes our way is what we want. I cannot count the women I know who feel they've been dealt a crummy hand, yet would rather play the cards they've been given than demand new ones. It's as if they're afraid the Cosmic Dealer will be angry with them if they ask for a better hand.

I just don't understand that.

If you're a woman who is more comfortable reacting to life than acting upon it, I am here to tell you that you get what you ask for and that if you don't ask, you're going to end up settling for less

> If you're a woman who is more comfortable reacting to life than acting upon it, I am here to tell you that you get what you ask for and that if you don't ask, you're going to end up settling for less than you want (and deserve).

than you want (and deserve). It's just the way life is: each of us is born into a set of circumstances—a family drama, you might say—and assigned a role. We are expected to play this role not because our parents have it in for us, or our sisters and brothers are luckier, or because we were born under an unfortunate alignment of the planets. We're expected to play that role because the people whose tribe we're born into—our family—are already living a certain way, and figure we'll live that way, too. And we often do. But the point is, we don't have to.

My philosophy as a woman is, and always has been, that I would not settle for a loveless marriage, or subsist as a second-class citizen, or sacrifice my health to the latest fads, or live according to society's definition of what a woman should be. I insist, and have always insisted, on defining myself by the choices I make, and I started making them when I was still in my teens.

My parents couldn't afford to send me away to college, so the plan was for me to work during the day so I could help pay the bills and take classes at night. The minute I graduated from high school I had to get a full-time job, so I went to work in the proof and transit department of a large bank downtown. My job was to cancel the checks that people had written by running them through a machine that stamped a row of numbers on the bottom. This was the early 1970s and there was no such thing as free checking; you had to pay a fee of twenty-five or even fifty cents for every check you wrote. I decided to go to work for the bank because, if you were an employee, they would process all your checks free of charge. My father was working sporadically at the time and not bringing in much money, so I had the bank deposit my salary directly into my checking account and I was able to pay our bills and cover any cash shortfalls that cropped up.

One day during my lunch hour, I stopped into a drugstore and ran into a girl named Brenda who had been in my high-school graduating class. I didn't know her well because we moved to Texas from Oklahoma the year before and I'd been at that high school for my senior year only. But we'd had a few classes together, so we said hello and visited for a while. It turned out that she was going to college in town, working part-time, and dating a man named Doug who was a pilot in the Air Force. She asked if I was dating anyone and when I told her I wasn't, she said Doug had a roommate who was also a pilot, and she would like to introduce me to him. She thought we'd get along, and then the four of us could double date.

This was late August and I'd been canceling checks full time for over three months, so a date with an Air Force pilot sounded pretty good. Brenda said she and Doug were going out that weekend and she invited me to spend the weekend with her at her parents' house, suggesting we head out on our date from there. So we exchanged phone numbers and had lunch together, and ended up having a lot of fun.

On Saturday afternoon I packed an overnight bag, told my parents where I was going, and headed over to Brenda's parents' house. We were up in her bedroom getting ready for our date and I was giggling and horsing around when she turned to me and started talking real low.

"You have to be quiet because my brother is in the room next door and he's very, very sick," she said. "The doctor's on his way to the house to see him." It sounded awfully serious.

"What's wrong with him?" I asked.

"We don't really know," she said. "We think it's pneumonia or something, but he's really sick and we have to be quiet." I told her okay, and then I thought for a minute.

"Brenda," I said, "I didn't even know you had a brother."

"Yeah, he's older than I am. He just came back into town this week."

So we went out that night and I met Doug's roommate, who was a nice enough guy. He asked me out for the following weekend and we decided I would spend the weekend at Brenda's again. But at the last minute he had to do some kind of pilot training exercise and broke our half of the date. Brenda and Doug invited me to join them but I didn't want to tag along, so Brenda suggested I hang out at her parents' house until she got back since I had planned to spend the night anyway. So she and Doug left and I went into the den to watch TV.

I remember I was wearing a T-shirt and cut-off blue jeans (back then that was the thing to wear—old, worn-out blue jeans that you cut into shorts, the shorter the better), and my hair was long and tied up in a ponytail. I didn't have any makeup on because my date had canceled, and I was sitting there watching TV when I saw this big guy coming down the hall toward the family room. He stopped in the doorway and stared at me. I remember I had a mouth full of sunflower seeds—the kind that come in the shells and you have to crack them with your teeth and spit out the hulls—and I looked at him and he looked at me and it dawned on me, *Oh, that's the brother. That's the brother.*

He looks at me and he says, "Who are you and what are you doing here?" He was all scruffy looking because he'd been sick in bed. His hair was sticking out, he hadn't shaved in days, and he was just not very friendly. I'll admit I was a bit intimidated, but there is something in me that thinks people should be polite to guests in their home. So I looked right back at him with a mouth full of sunflower seeds and a head full of indignation.

"What do you mean, who am I?" I said. "Who are *you?*"

"I'm Phil, Brenda's brother," he said.

"Oh, you've been sick."

"Yes."

"Brenda says you've been sick for a long time. How are you feeling?"

"Fine." (You can see who was carrying the conversation.)

"Oh, wow," I said. "I was here the day the doctor came. What was wrong with you?" Once I start talking, I talk a lot. I really do. I started asking him about what he'd had and how he felt, all the while cracking those sunflower seeds in my mouth (I was addicted to sunflower seeds that year; I ate them all the time). And he sat down and studied me and we sat for hours and visited; and I asked him a ton of questions and found out everything I wanted to know. (Hey—he was cute, I was interested, I needed information, and I was going after what I wanted.)

I found out that he was going to be a junior in college, but he was a little older because he'd taken a leave of absence to recover from football injuries he'd gotten as a freshman at the University of Tulsa. Along the way he had become a partner in a health club, made it a huge success, sold off his share, used the money to buy a string of other clubs, gotten married, taken a year's worth of classes at Texas Tech, sold off all the health clubs, and gotten divorced. (I'm a cracker-jack interviewer, aren't I?) He also had his pilot's license, which he had gotten at the age of sixteen. Oh yes—and he owned his own plane.

I was impressed. Most of the college students I knew didn't own their own cars; this guy owned a *plane*. He said it wasn't fancy or anything; in fact, he made it sound like a flying jalopy. But hey— any twenty-one-year-old who owned his own plane had to be doing something right, and I remember thinking that was pretty cool.

I also remember thinking he was huge. My father was a small man, very lean and wiry, and my brother isn't real tall either. In fact, most of my family is pretty slender and small, so that's what I was used to. But the men in Phillip's family tend to shop in the he-man department. He was 6'4" and about 235 pounds, very muscular; he filled up the doorway, and I wasn't used to that. I'm not easily frightened, but I've got to tell you, he scared me to death, because he wasn't very outgoing, at least not right away. He seemed very different from Brenda, who was friendly and quick to smile (and still is). And I'll break into a smile at anything or for anyone, so Phillip's "non-smiley-ness" was a challenge for me.

I must have made some headway, though, because when I told him I'd never been in an airplane, he offered to take me up for a spin the following evening. That was our first date, and we've been together ever since—except for when we broke up (I'll get to that later).

At some point early on, though, I looked at him and said, "Phillip, you're going to have to lighten up. Because if we're going to be together and get married and live the rest of our lives together, we're going to have fun. You're just way too serious." And he did lighten up a bit and learn to have some fun. But he's still at heart a serious and focused person. He's very intense and stoic, and to this day he has a hard time showing excitement. I remember when he signed his first book contract, I was jumping around and turning cartwheels in the kitchen. And he was standing there saying, "Yeah, it's good, it's good." And I was jumping out of my skin, saying, "Come on, honey, this is a big deal. Give me a 'whoopee' or something!" And he smiled, but that's as far as it went. It's not that he wasn't excited about getting the contract; he was, and I knew it because I could see it in his face. He's just not the type of man who shows what he's feeling—good or bad.

He's got a strong sense of humor, though, which comes out sometimes during the show. He's hilarious but he's also deadpan; you can't always tell he's joking from the look on his face. But he's a funny, funny man, and I love to see him laugh. And I do, often, because he melts when he's around me. He thinks I've got a smart-alecky sense of humor—spunky, he calls it—and I don't hold back, because I love to make him smile.

When Phillip was voted one of *People* magazine's sexiest men, they interviewed me and asked when I thought he was at his sexiest. And I said, "When I make him laugh," because he has the sweetest smile, and when he smiles it shows in his eyes and his playful side comes through. If I say something funny, he cannot keep from laughing, and I think that's very sexy. Because here's this big, strong man who can't keep from laughing because of *me*; it's like I have this power over him—the power of joy—as I had with my father, and it makes me feel close and connected to him.

But I will say this: he doesn't scare me anymore. As intense and as serious as he can get, I don't let him get the best of me. I hang in there, and I give as good as I get. I think that's another part of what makes our marriage work: we are evenly matched. He's intense, I'm forthright. He's serious, I'm exuberant. He's introspective, I'm expressive. He's scientific, I'm artistic. And it works very well for us.

I had a sense of it that first night in the McGraws' family room, that this was the man for me. You know how you just know something, sometimes? That's how it was when I met Phillip: as big as he was, as serious and just plain different as he was, I knew that we were meant for each other. All that I had to do was make him see it that way, too.

We became very close very quickly. He had one more year of college to go and began classes a few weeks after we met. I continued to work at the bank until the end of the year, when I changed jobs and went to work at Western Auto Supply, a kind of low-end department store that carried automotive equipment and household appliances. I was the credit manager and sat at a desk and checked people's credit when they came in and wanted to buy something big like a washing machine or a refrigerator on time. It was a very plain place, with fluorescent lights and linoleum floors and customers who looked as if they couldn't rub two nickels together. To hear Phillip describe it, you'd think it was the most depressing place on earth, which it may have been. But I didn't dwell on that at the time; all I knew was that I was the credit manager, I was earning a decent wage, and I was dating someone I was in love with.

We'd see each other most nights; Phillip would study and I would read or work on something else I was involved in. Phillip was always very disciplined and approached his education with the same singularity of purpose that I would later see him bring to his career. He treated school as if it were a job: he read textbooks as soon as they were assigned, completed assignments before they were due, and studied with the focus of someone who knew that doing so would bring him that much closer to his goal.

Meanwhile, I was focused on my own goal. As I said earlier, I knew I was meant to be a wife and mother, and by this point I knew Phillip was the man whose wife I was meant to be. I felt pretty sure that he wanted me, too, but he was deeply involved in getting his bachelor's degree, and I knew that his education was his top priority (as well it should have been). I also knew better than to distract him from it, so I would have to sit tight, let him do his thing, and make sure I was around when he took study breaks.

One thing he did break for was to play tennis several times a week because it helped him stay in shape and blow off steam. So one day he asked me if I played tennis. My mind started working at warp speed. I had never held a tennis racquet in my life, but if I told him that he wouldn't play with me because he was too skilled to have patience with a beginner and too busy to teach me. So, eyes on the prize, I did what I had to do. "Yes, I play!" I said, "Absolutely, sure!" And I'm thinking, *If I have to learn tonight, I will,* because if learning to play tennis in twenty-four hours meant I could be with him and we could have some fun, I would be Billie Jean King by sunrise. (She had recently trounced Bobby Riggs in a widely publicized match at the Houston Astrodome that Riggs had arranged to prove the alleged superiority of male players. I figured if she could demolish a blowhard like Riggs with a racquet, I could learn to hit a ball with one.)

But Phillip did me one better and said, "Okay. Let's go out and hit some!" Like, right that minute. And I said, "Great! Let's go."

Now, before you write me off as a cheat and a liar, let me explain. First, he was testing me, and I knew it. Second, you know as well as I do that sometimes a gal's got to do what a gal's got to do. And I absolutely had to get out there on the tennis court and make a fool of myself. (It was a small price to pay to be with my man, you know?)

So we went out there and I could hardly even hold the racket. I'm running around and flapping it like a butterfly net.

"You can't play!" Phillip said.

"No, I can't," I replied. "But aren't we having fun? And don't I look cute in these shorts?"

And he got this adorable look on his face and said, "Yeah, you're right. You're right." And I told myself, *There you go, Robin. You just do whatever it takes.*

Another time when Phillip and I were dating, I remember wanting to do something to make him happy, so I asked him, "Do you like pie?"

"Oh yeah," he said. "I love pie. Love pie."

"What's your favorite?"

"Chocolate cream pie."

"Ooh, I'm a good baker," I said. "I make a great chocolate cream pie."

"Oh, really?"

"Really. I'll make you one."

I still lived at home with my parents and my mother could bake anything. So I told her the story and she said, "I'm going to make Phil a pie and you can give it to him." (Yes, she was an enabler, but boy, could she bake.) And the whole time she was making that pie, I was watching her like a hawk. And I'd call Phillip and say, "Okay, honey, I'm rolling out the crust now. Sweetie, I'm spooning in the chocolate now, mm-mmm, that's good!" And I would describe exactly what she was doing. And he would say, "Oh, really? Uh-huh, uh-huh." (He does the same thing on the *Dr. Phil* show when a guest says something and he isn't really buying it. He doesn't want to say so, so he looks down at his blue note cards and does this little "uh-huh" thing.)

So he'd do that on the phone and I'd say, "Okay, I'm whipping up the filling . . . Okay, I just put it in the oven . . . Okay, it's coming out . . . Ooh, it's out and it's cooling, and I'm whipping the cream." And finally, "I'm about to shave a little chocolate on top . . . guess what, honey? I'm coming over!" I loaded the pie onto a plate and took it over to his house.

"So, what do you think of my pie?" I said. "Doesn't it look good?" I was laying it on thick. Then, as he was savoring the first bite I took the plunge.

"I didn't really make it," I said. "My mother did."

"Yeah, I knew that," he said. And to this day he swears he knew that my mother was baking the pie and that he took all my phone calls just so he wouldn't spoil the surprise. Which is exactly right: I didn't lie to deceive him; I just wanted to surprise him and please him. I did a lot of that, surprising him and pleasing him and doing little things to show how I felt about him.

I did big things, too, like moving out of my parents' house and following him to Denton when he left for the University of North Texas to start graduate school. We had been dating almost two years, and although we weren't ready to get engaged, we did want to be together. There was no reason for me not to go with him and moreover, I felt it was time to leave home. So Phillip and I decided I would move to Denton, get a job, and go to school at night.

I found a small apartment not too far from Phillip's place, and I also found a terrific job as the Unicom operator at Denton Municipal Airport, which meant I gave landing instructions to pilots when they wanted to fly in. It was a small private airport and a very busy one, so I handled the air traffic and pretty much ran the office as well. Plus I was taking college classes at night, so I was never bored. In the evenings Phillip and I would either meet at the university library or hang out at his apartment or mine and study. He was very focused on his schoolwork because he had quit school once already and ended up running a business, so he didn't want anything to distract him from completing his Ph.D. And I understood and supported that 100 percent.

We had been there about a year when I began to feel strongly that I wanted to be married. Phillip and I spent all our nonworking time together, just like a married couple, only we lived in different places. There was no question about our commitment to each other, and it seemed to me that enough time had passed for us both to know what we were getting into. So I took a deep breath one night and put it out there.

"Phillip," I said, "we need to make a decision about where we're going with this. We've been together about three years now, and I would like to get married." He closed his book, cleared his throat, and looked into my eyes.

"Robin," he said, "I can't get married yet. I'm just not ready. I really feel I need to finish my education first. I can't stop like I did last time and go into business and all that. I'm so focused on finishing this program that I don't want to commit to you until I can give 100 percent to being married. I'm not going to get married until I can do that."

I let it sink in for a moment and then I spoke.

"You know what?" I said. "I put my cards on the table and you chose not to play the hand. But now I know how you feel, and I'm out of here." I stacked up my books, put on my coat, and left.

It was probably the smartest thing I've ever done.

I was very serious about getting what I wanted and what I needed. And as much as I cared for him, I cared for myself just as much and I thought, *I am not going to be strung along here.* I was a really good girlfriend; I took really good care of him. I had devoted three years to showing him who I was and what life would be like if he chose me for his bride, and I wanted to know that we were going to get married. I thought this was perfectly reasonable (and I was right).

As disappointed as I was that my boyfriend wouldn't commit, I didn't hold it against him. I knew it wasn't because he didn't love me. I respected Phillip's position, which was that he had made a commitment to himself to get his Ph.D. and nothing was going to stop him. But I had also made a commitment to myself and respected myself enough to not let anything stop me, either. I've always been the type that once I've made up my mind, that's it. I'm an all-or-nothing person, which in some ways is good and in some ways is bad. But, good or bad, I have strong convictions, and I stand by them.

So we broke up. The next day I went up to Beverly, who worked at the airport with me, and told her if she still needed a place to live she could share mine. I was feeling a bit lonely and thought she would be good company, not to mention a big help with the rent. So by the end of the week I had a roommate and some extra spending money.

This was the fall of 1975. I was not quite twenty-two, nor was I quite ready to give up on the idea of marrying Phillip McGraw (just because I broke up with him didn't mean I didn't want him). So I waited a respectable interval after our break-up—about two months—until I knew he was back home for the holidays, and I phoned his parents' house. Phillip and I had not spoken since the night I told him I was out of there, and I knew he had to be missing me. But I didn't want to talk to him just yet. So I picked a time he was likely to be out, called him at his parents' house, and left a message for him to call me. (I may even have been in cahoots with Brenda or his mother to find out for certain when he'd be out; I don't remember.) I wanted to call when he wouldn't be there so I could tantalize him with an "I wondered if you could call me" message. I knew he would call back.

And he did. I had Beverly answer even though I was sitting right there—these were the days before caller I.D., so I asked her to answer all our phone calls so I wouldn't get caught by surprise. She said, "Oh, sorry. Robin's not here, she's out on a date."

And he said, "Ohhh . . ." I could hear it; I had my ear next to the receiver while she was talking. Then she very politely took a message and hung up.

He called back a few days later and this time I got on the phone. He said, "Hi, you know, I'm coming back from winter break in a couple of weeks and I'm going to be flying in on a Friday night just as you're getting off work. So could we maybe go to dinner and see each other?"

"Sure," I said, just as cool as could be. And he gave me the tail number of his airplane—5902Q (I can't believe I still remember that)—and I hung up the phone. I was so excited, I could not sit down for a good half-hour.

So the big night finally came. I was at work at the airport and when he called in from his plane, my roommate turned to me and said, "Here he is, here he is!" And I gave him the landing instructions and saw him taxi in, and he timed it perfectly, just as I was getting off work. We got in the car and went to dinner and then went back to his apartment, where we sat and talked. And we both admitted that we loved each other and missed each other, and that neither of us wanted anybody else.

And he asked me to marry him, and I said yes (big surprise). This was in the middle of January 1976, and a month later, on Valentine's Day, he gave me an engagement ring. We got married six months later to the day, on August 14, 1976, which happened to be the day he was supposed to attend graduation for his master's degree. But he said—and I thought this was significant—that the master's wasn't a big deal because he was continuing in the doctoral program, so he would just as soon spend the day at his wedding as at his graduation. And I thought that was so sweet of him, giving our wedding priority over his graduation; it was a symbolic gesture, a gift to me. So as his classmates were walking across the stage getting diplomas, he was walking down the aisle.

> I believe that God means for me to be an advocate for myself, both in my marriage and every other aspect of my life.

Not incidentally, I was getting what I wanted, too. And I had gotten it on my terms.

I have said repeatedly that I believe that I was put on this earth to be Phillip's wife and I believe that God meant for us to be together. But I also believe that God means for me to be an advocate for myself, both in my marriage and every other aspect of my life. And no one agrees with me more than Phillip. As he says, we teach people how to treat us, and that night over thirty years ago in his apartment, I taught him that he could not treat me like a comfy old pair of shoes that gathers dust in the closet. I taught him that if we were going to be together, it would have to be on my terms as well as his.

It's interesting: when I tell this story to women, they cheer when I tell them I walked out. And then they ask, "Weren't you worried he'd go out and find someone else?" And the answer is, "No, I was not," for two reasons. First, I knew that he loved me. Second, if he were to go out and find somebody else without coming after me or fighting for me, then he was clearly not as crazy about me as I wanted my husband to be. Besides, it's not as if I sat passively by, grieving for this great love that might have been. I called him, after all. I chased him until he caught me. I didn't like living without him while we were broken up, but, as I said before, sometimes a gal's got to do what a gal's got to do. And I'll do whatever it takes.

Which is how I got maybe the best job I ever had.

After we were married and Phillip got his doctorate, he was assigned to a psychology internship at a veteran's hospital in Waco, about 115 miles south of Denton. I had left my airport job for an even better one as executive assistant to the CEO of a vending machine manufacturing company, but now we were moving and I'd have to find a new job.

As it happened, Phillip's sister Donna and her husband, Scott, lived in Waco. (Phillip has three sisters, Brenda, Donna, and Deana.) Scott now works for the *Dr. Phil* show, but at the time he was an industrial engineer for a company that manufactured and packaged surgical supplies. When Scott heard we'd be moving down there, he told Phillip of an opening in his department for a technician. Scott thought I'd be great at it, so he invited us down that weekend so he could explain the job to me, and said he'd set me up for an interview for Monday.

Why not? I'd never been an industrial engineering technician, but I was a quick learner. So we flew down to Waco, Donna and Scott had us over to dinner, and Scott prepped me for the interview. He said the job would require me to design the most efficient way to stock various kinds of surgical packs, which are containers of sterile supplies used in operating rooms. I would have to come up with a different process for each pack, depending on the kind of procedure it was meant to serve. For instance, a gall bladder pack would contain the specific kinds of gauze, ties, clamps, and other paraphernalia needed for that kind of operation, while a Cesarean section pack would include the sponges and ties needed for abdominal surgery as well as an umbilical cord clamp and nasal syringe for the baby.

Scott said I would be interviewed by a panel of men and gave me a few pointers on the kinds of abilities they might be looking for. He said he would be at the interview but would not say anything to me because we agreed that it was entirely up to me to convince them I was capable of doing the job. I agreed that this was right, and thanked him for all he'd done. The bottom line was I had to go into that interview and convince those men that I'd be a crackerjack industrial engineering technician.

The next morning, I was ushered into a room to meet with the six-man interviewing committee. They explained that the job would require me to create packaging procedures, run time studies to determine the most cost-efficient ones, analyze the results to set incentive pay rates for the hourly employees who would assemble the packs, and write up the instructions for the procedure that was deemed most efficient. I nodded confidently as they explained the various aspects of the job.

Then this one man said, "We use a packing protocol that implements a set number of steps as dictated by our corporate guidelines. How many steps were implemented by the packing protocol at your former job?"

I had to think fast. I was working for a company that made vending machines, so I thought, *Okay: how many steps does it take to put together and stock a vending machine?* A number popped into my head and I decided to go with it. I looked him straight in the eye.

"Two hundred."

He looked at me as if to say, "What?!" Scott's eyes got big and round, and I thought to myself, *Uh-oh, I guess that's not the answer they're looking for.* So I smiled brightly and (never one to be at a loss for words) said, "Oh, I'm so sorry, I misunderstood. The answer is five—we use a *five*-step process." And the man said, "Oh, that's better, that makes sense."

Whew! I could feel the adrenaline tingling through every nerve cell in my body, but I wasn't going to just sit on a wrong answer. Hey, I believe in the old saying, "Never let 'em see you sweat!" I got the job.

I loved that job. It challenged my mind and made the most of my organizational abilities, which my family can tell you are off the charts—just give me a new house with an empty kitchen, and I'll stock those drawers and cupboards better than any efficiency expert could do it. If you need efficiency, I'm your gal, and that's what the job called for. I knew they needed me even if it took a little convincing for them to know it.

I immersed myself in the finer points of assembling surgical packs and set about designing efficient ways to do it. It took some ingenuity, because the supplies had to be inserted into the pack in the opposite order from which they would be needed in the operating room; for instance, the suturing material used to close an incision at the end of a surgery would be one of the first things you'd place in the pack because it would be one of the last things the surgeon would need.

Then came the time studies, which required me to walk around and time assembly-line employees while they filled the packs, with the purpose of determining how many they could fill in an hour working at a reasonably brisk pace. Then, if someone exceeded that number, he or she would get a bonus—called "incentive pay"—for producing more. I would walk around with a large clipboard-type contraption with four stopwatches attached to it, and time how long it took the workers to complete each step of the process. I would compute the number of seconds or minutes it took each worker to do each of the four steps, determine the average amount of time it took to do them, and compute the average time it took to complete the four-step process. I was then able to determine how many units a worker would need to assemble in an hour to qualify for incentive pay.

What a joy! It may not sound exciting to others, but to me it was heaven. I learned a lot from that job—about medicine and surgery, and the stuff that goes on during an operation that the patient never sees. Best of all, I learned about the soul-satisfying pleasure of working at something you're good at. I'll always have a soft spot in my heart for Scott for setting up that interview, and for those six guys who decided to hire me. They clearly saw something that persuaded them to take a chance on me, and I'll always be grateful that they gave me the opportunity to shine.

They say that luck is what happens when preparation meets opportunity, and I know it's true. A lot of things seem to go right for me, and it's not because I'm more deserving than other people; it's because I put a lot of energy into making things happen. I'm a great believer in the power of energy—the force that emerges when you set your mind to accomplishing something—and what happens when you use it as a catalyst. Things may not always turn out the way you imagined they would, but that's not the point. The point is to look inside yourself, identify what you need to be happy, and to put things in motion to secure that happiness.

Which is how I came to acquire a Brownie troop.

Phillip was in graduate school and I was working during the day and taking classes at night. We were living in a little house and were not exactly flush; I brought in about $250 a week and Phillip's teaching assistantship netted him about $300 a month, so we didn't go out much. I studied, did things around the house, learned to cook, and took care of us. Phillip and I didn't see all that much of each other because he was studying whenever he wasn't in class;

plus, he went away one weekend a month to see patients with his father, who had a thriving psychotherapy practice of his own.

I have always loved children and was looking forward to having a few of my own. But we barely had enough money to support ourselves and Phillip was adamant about not starting a family until we had more coming in. Phillip is staunchly conservative when it comes to finances: if he can't pay cash in full, he won't buy it. So, whereas I knew we'd have to wait a few years to have kids of our own, what was to stop me from having kids around who weren't my own?

This is exactly what I had in mind when I picked up the phone and called the local chapter of the Girls Scouts of America and told the woman who answered that I loved little girls and wanted to lead a Brownie troop. She was delighted. "How wonderful!" she said. "We always need leaders. What school does your daughter attend?"

"Actually, I don't have children," I said. "Not yet. I'm married and my husband's a graduate student in psychology and we're going to start a family when he graduates."

"You don't have children, but you want to lead a Brownie troop?"

"Yes, ma'am. I sure do."

"I don't believe we've ever had a request quite like yours. You'll have to come down to the office."

I had to go in for an interview so they wouldn't think I was a lunatic, and I had to prove that I really wanted to be a Brownie leader even though I didn't have any children. And I must have done okay because they said there was a school that needed a leader for a bunch of girls in kindergarten and first grade. They'd let me create and lead a troop as long as I understood that I was on probation, and they'd be checking up to see how I was doing. And I said, great!

I had eight little girls and they would all come to the house and I would run arts and crafts activities. The organization had guidelines we had to follow for the girls to earn their badges, so I did everything just so (I was on probation, after all). At one of our meetings, I remember reading aloud from the official Girl Scout newsletter that kept leaders updated on programs and activities. And I got to the part about the annual Girl Scout jamboree, when they all get together for a few nights and go camping, and these little girls all started cheering and clapping because they were so excited.

So I'm reading aloud about all the fun they're going to have and I get to the fine print: the overnight camping trip isn't open to Brownie troops. And I stop in the middle of the sentence and say, "Wait a minute, girls, you're too young. We can't do this." And they look up at me with these pitiful faces and they all start to cry. I thought, *Oh, my gosh, what have I done?* It was so pathetic; one minute they were all cheering and the next they were sobbing around my kitchen table. So I said, "Okay, here's the deal; we'll have our own jamboree right here. We'll camp out in my backyard next weekend—how's that?" And don't you know, they were cheering again.

What I didn't realize was that Phillip would be out of town the following weekend, so I would have to run the jamboree on my own. But I had an idea. We lived next door to a wonderful couple, Ronnie and Diane. They were older and a bit like surrogate parents to Phillip and me. Ronnie's family owned a grave digging business, so Ronnie was the person who would come out to the cemetery before a burial to dig the grave and set up a tent to shelter the family if the weather was bad. I called him and said, "Ronnie, I'm going to have a bunch of kids camped out in my backyard next weekend and Phillip won't be here; how do I set up a tent?"

"Don't worry," he said. "I'll handle it." And he put up a funeral tent to shelter my Brownies.

The following Saturday afternoon, eight cars pulled up to the house, and out popped eight little girls with sleeping bags, pillows, and Barbie dolls galore. I had planned all kinds of games and they were having a ball. Ronnie and Diane helped me feed them and when it began to get dark, the girls and I piled into our sleeping bags and snuggled up together. I read them stories and we had flashlights and marshmallows, and they eventually got drowsy and fell asleep.

I did too but was awakened a few hours later by the pitter-patter of raindrops that soon became a deluge. There I was, three o'clock in the morning under a funeral tent with eight groggy little girls, and it's lightning and they're squealing and I'm saying, "Girls, we're going to have to go into the house." Their sleeping bags were wet, so I ran to the linen closet, grabbed every sheet and blanket I owned (including the ones from our bed), and made pallets on the floor. Despite my best efforts, two girls were scared to death and crying, so I had to call their parents to come get them in the middle of the night. I was drenched and thought I would keel over with exhaustion. It was one of the best nights of my life.

The next morning dawned bright and clear, and I had six little angels sleeping on the living room floor in my little house; it was just adorable. I loved leading that Brownie troop because I got to do what I love to do: spend time with children and put my energies into making them happy. And it's funny, because when I pictured myself as a mother, I always pictured myself as having boys. It had always been my dream to have sons, which is what I ended up having. But these were girls, and I could not have enjoyed them more. They were exactly whom I needed to be with at that point in my life, and I consider it a blessing and a privilege to have been the first childless Brownie troop leader in Waco, Texas.

> To me, there's a huge difference between expecting happiness to come to you because you deserve it, and going out and getting the happiness you believe you deserve.

I've thought about that Brownie troop many times since I last saw them (those little girls must be well into their thirties by now!), and what tickles me most about the whole experience is that I did it in the first place. I knew very well that troop leaders were typically the mothers of girls in the scouting program, but that didn't stop me. I knew that I wanted to work with children and that I'd have to find a part-time way of doing it. The Girl Scouts seemed like a good match so I pursued them, and we turned out to be perfect for each other.

As soon as I know I want something to happen in my life, I start thinking and acting as if that much-desired thing is just around the corner, waiting for me to come and launch it into being. Like with the Brownies; I knew I loved children and wanted to be around them, so I had a choice: I could either mope around because I didn't have kids of my own, or I could be around somebody else's.

It's one of the oldest sayings around, but I tend to believe that the Lord helps those who help themselves, and I've never hesitated to help myself to happiness when it's available. And it's available everywhere, if only people would see it. That's the thing: people don't see the potential they have for happiness because, on some level, they think they're as happy as they deserve to be, no matter how unhappy they are. To me, there's a huge difference between expecting happiness to come to you because you deserve it, and going out and getting the happiness you believe you deserve. I know so many people who say, "I think I'm a good person; I guess I'm happy." To me, that is not a ringing expression of self-worth. You have to believe in your heart that you deserve to be happy, and then, when you have the happiness you want, you have to be aware of it and appreciate it.

A lot of people have a great life, but they just don't see it. They choose to focus not on what they actually have but on what they believe they lack, and they miss what life is all about. Some people never have enough; no matter how devoted their mate is, they always wish he (or she) were fitter, richer, or more attractive. No matter how accomplished their kids are, they always think they could have won a bigger trophy or higher academic honor if only they'd tried a little harder. No matter how nice their car or how gracious their home, they always want a bigger or a fancier model.

And while I firmly believe in striving for a good life, I also believe you've got to recognize when you've got it good, and thank God for what you've got.

I have a good life. I wake up every morning in my wonderful home and thank God for all the joy and abundance with which He has blessed me. But, while I love this house, it is not what makes me wake up happy every day. If Phillip and I were not solid in our commitment to each other, this house wouldn't do us a lick of good; it would just be a bigger space in which to be lonely.

It doesn't matter where we live; we started out in a one-bedroom apartment, and I could go back there today. I swear to you I could leave this 90210 lifestyle, throw on some cut-off jeans and a T-shirt, and go back to that little apartment in Denton, Texas, with my husband. We'd be just as happy as we could be, as long as we were together and proud of each other and doing what was important.

Yes, I love the mosaic floors and crystal chandeliers in this house, but not any more than a certain pair of wooden barstools that graced our apartment when Phillip was in grad school. I'll never forget this. He was off working with his father for the weekend and I decided I was going to do something fun with the apartment and surprise him when he got back. I had eight dollars left over from that week's budget to play around with, so I went to the supermarket and bought a can of tangerine orange paint and a brush for five dollars, and a little ivy plant with the three dollars I had left. I came home to our bland little apartment with the beige walls and brown carpet and painted these two bar stools a bright tangerine color and set them next to the breakfast bar where they glowed like a Tahitian sunset. I took the green ivy and set it on the bar so it cascaded off the edge onto the seat of that shimmering barstool, and I thought it was the most beautiful thing I had ever seen. And in many ways, it still is. Its preciousness transcended the eight dollars it cost me to create it, because it was born in my heart and made real by my hands. I imagined it and made it happen. To me, there's nothing better.

Chapter 5

A DISCERNING HEART

What I Learned from My Mother's
Legacy of Love

You never know when your life will change forever. One moment your existence is tidy and ordered with everything and everyone in its place; then a tornado blows through and life as you knew it lies scattered around you, tattered and broken and making no sense at all. Sometimes you can see it coming and can prepare yourself; other times it's over before you know what hit you and all you can do is stand there, dazed and shell-shocked, and try to make sense of the new reality you must absorb and accept.

That's what happened to me one Sunday morning over twenty years ago when my mother died. I had no warning, no time to prepare. All I had was the sound of her voice and the incomprehensible realization, later, that I would never hear it again. One moment she was talking to me; the next moment there was silence. It was swift and it was final, and I didn't know what hit me—or her—until later.

The day would have been memorable in any case because it was the first morning in our new home. The moving van had left only hours before, in the middle of a rainy night that had transformed my neatly packed boxes into sagging cardboard mounds. We were thrilled to move into the new house—which was actually an old house crosstown from where we'd been living before—but it happened much faster than we'd planned. We had been living

> One moment she was talking to me; the next moment there was silence. It was swift and it was final, and I didn't know what hit me—or her—until later.

in a beautiful place we'd built ourselves, but now that Jay was starting kindergarten we wanted to move into a different neighborhood in an older section of town. It had big, old houses, huge trees, and good schools, which made the neighborhood both highly desirable and pricey. So we figured we'd look for an old place we could afford and fix it up.

I went out and found just what we were looking for: a big old house with a lot of potential. Almost everything inside the house needed to be changed, but the price was right. Besides, I love taking an old house and making it my own. Whenever we move into a new place Phillip says, "It won't smell like home until it smells like you." I wear perfume and spray it around the house, I light candles, I cook and bake cakes; these are things I've always done that make our house smell like home. Phillip loves that, and when I saw that dreary, dusty old house, I thought, *Just wait 'till I get my hands on this place; I'll make it a beautiful home.*

So we made an offer on the house and put our relatively new one on the market. And, wouldn't you know it, the first person who came to look at our place offered us the asking price in cash. So we sold it, just like that, and had three whole weeks to pack up and get out. I got the keys to the new place and went to work painting the bedrooms and fixing up the kitchen just enough to make them livable. We started packing and calling movers but the only time anyone could fit us in was on a Saturday after another job.

So in the dark of an October evening, in the pouring rain, a moving crew arrived and loaded our furniture into two eighteen-wheelers. It was still raining and past three in the morning by the time the last box was unloaded, and at some point just before dawn Phillip and I decided to go to bed. Jay was spending the night at a friend's house, and I wanted to get a few hours' sleep before he returned. I was also expecting my mother and wanted to unpack the kitchen a bit before she got there. She had called while the movers were loading up and offered to come over in the morning and help me unpack, but I had said, "You know, mother, instead of coming over bright and early, would you bake me one of your pumpkin pies and bring it over so I'll have a treat while I'm unpacking?" She said she'd be happy to.

We awoke at about ten o'clock the next morning to a clear blue sky, an appetite for breakfast, and nothing to eat in the house. Phillip threw on some clothes and headed out to the grocery store to pick up some donuts. I was busy unpacking a box when the phone rang. I always like the first phone call in a new house, and my mother was the only person who had our new number so I knew it was her.

"Good morning," she said. "How's the new house?"

"It's old," I said, "and my boxes are wet and it doesn't smell very good in here. Which reminds me. How's my pie coming?"

"I just took it out of the oven. As soon as it cools, I'll bring it over," she said.

"Ooh, that's great—I can't wait." She was quiet for a moment.

"Robin, is Phil there?"

"No, he went out for some donuts. Why?"

"Oh," my mother said, "I feel kind of funny. I just wanted to ask him about it."

"What do you mean by funny?"

Silence. The line went dead.

I thought we had gotten disconnected and I hung up. At that moment, Phillip walked in and the phone started ringing again.

"That must be my mother," I said. "We got disconnected and she wants to ask you something." So Phillip picked up the phone and from where I was standing I could hear my father's voice crackling, "Oh my God! Something's happened, something's happened to Georgia! Help me, help me!"

Phillip said, "Jim, listen to me. Hang up the phone right now and call an ambulance. We'll be right there."

We jumped in the car and raced over to my parents' house. I ran to the bedroom and saw my mother lying across the bed, her face a sickly grayish-blue. Phillip ran to her and started doing CPR. He actually got her breathing again and some color returned to her face. I heard a siren growing closer, then distant, then closer again, and realized the ambulance couldn't find my parents' little street and thought how horrible it was that she might die while it was trying to find the house. Then Phillip was working on her again and I watched in horror, not knowing what to say, what to do, what to think. Everything was happening too quickly and too slowly, all at the same time.

My father was becoming frantic, so I took him outside to flag down the ambulance. It arrived moments later, and paramedics crashed into the house and back toward the bedroom. Phillip stepped back and the paramedics took over, continuing CPR while they transferred her to a gurney, while Phillip said something to them that I couldn't hear.

As they were wheeling her outside, Phillip suggested I ride in the ambulance, thinking it might give me a few precious moments with my mother were she to regain consciousness. I climbed in and she was hooked up to this machine, and I remember the high-pitched b-e-e-p it was making, shrill and steady like on television when the patient dies and the paramedic says, "I've lost her again."

I jumped out of that ambulance like I'd been shot. I just couldn't sit there and watch her die, so Phillip and I followed the ambulance in our car. I was in a state of emotional shock, and I kept asking Phillip, "Why aren't they speeding? Why aren't they running the sirens? What's wrong with them?" Phillip knew why they weren't tearing through traffic but drove on silently, holding my hand.

We got to the hospital and because Phillip was on staff he was able to get a small private room for us to wait in. I had already called Roger and he and his wife showed up shortly after we arrived. I had also called my sisters—Jamie, Karin, and Cindi— who were on their way. Cindi lived a bit of a distance away, so I was worried she might not get there in time to see mother. They had been particularly close and I knew Cindi would be devastated if she didn't have a chance to say good-bye.

I remember sitting in that little room and telling Phillip, "Go see if she's okay. Go see if she's okay." Of course, my mother wasn't okay; she had died of a massive heart attack while she was on the phone with me; she was only fifty-eight. Phillip knew she was gone all the time he had been giving her CPR, and what he'd been quietly telling the paramedics was that they should not pronounce my mother dead there in the bedroom but wait until they had moved her out of the house. Phillip knows that I'm a strong woman and can handle anything, but as a psychologist and the person in the world who knows me best, he knew that I would forever associate that house with my mother's death if she were pronounced there. He also knew I was going to need time to absorb the loss, which is why he secured a room for us to gather and wait in before breaking the news to us. In truth, my father and brother needed the time as much as I did, so we sat together in that room, fearing the worst yet praying for a miracle.

A woman's cry shocked us alert. I ran into the hall and saw Cindi in the waiting room, her coat still on, doubled over and gripping the edge of a molded plastic chair and crying as her heart broke.

It was then that I knew my mother was gone. My other sister Karin was with her, silent and stunned. I ran over and asked what had happened. Karin said that she had arrived at the emergency room just as Cindi was walking up to the nurse's station. When Cindi asked, "Where is Mrs. Jameson?" the nurse replied, "Oh, the woman who died awhile ago?" thinking that Cindi was from the funeral home. That's how Cindi learned our mother had died.

I put my arm around Cindi and led her back to the waiting room. It's curious that I'm the baby sister, but it was I who was comforting her. I'm the one who tends to take over the caretaker role, and my sisters know to expect that from me, even though I'm the youngest. Cindi especially, which is particularly odd because she babied Roger and me when we were little, as if we were her dolls. But I trust my judgment and believe that if I take control of things they will work out better than if I let them run their course. So it seemed completely natural that I would comfort Cindi and lead her and Karin back to the room.

We sat down and waited for reality to sink in. By this time Jamie had arrived and we were all sobbing and holding one another and trying to wrap our minds around the terrible thought that we would never see our mother alive again. I was especially distraught because I had been talking to her when it happened, whining and carrying on about my smelly house all the time she was dying. Every time I thought about her working on that pie while her heart was exploding, I'd break down and start shaking and sobbing all over again. So Phillip quietly stepped out to a pay phone and called his mother to ask her to come down and be with me. She and I were very close (and still are), and he knew it would bring me comfort to have her there.

Fifteen minutes later, Grandma Jerry walked into the room and called my name. And I looked up and cried, "Oh, Grandma, my mother has died! My mother is gone! She's gone!"

That dear, sweet woman took two steps toward me and collapsed with a heart attack.

I am telling the truth.

They rushed Phillip's mother upstairs to the coronary care unit while I watched, stunned and unmoving. The attack was a mild one, and Grandma was soon out of danger. I couldn't help but feel that I was somehow responsible and was shaken by the thought that I'd almost lost two mothers in one day.

I looked down and studied the floor. What world was this? How had I gotten here? I recognized my father and my sisters and my brother and my husband, and yet I knew no one. Everyone looked the same, yet everything was different. My mother was dead and Phillip's mother was in the CCU; it couldn't be and yet it was. What would happen to my father? How would he survive without my mother? What would I do? What would we all do?

> And something inside me said, *I will survive this . . . I will survive this.* I just knew. I believe that God doesn't give you more than you can handle, and I allowed myself to hold fast to that. I told myself, *Robin, there's a reason for this, and He knows you can handle it.*

And something inside me said, *I will survive this . . . I will survive this.* I just knew. I believe that God doesn't give you more than you can handle, and I allowed myself to hold fast to that. I told myself, *Robin, there's a reason for this, and He knows you can handle it.*

We pulled ourselves together and returned to the house in total shock. We started phoning family members and within hours, people started arriving at the house—which, you may recall, we had moved into less than twenty-fours hours before. Phillip and I shoved cartons against walls and cleared floor space so people could circulate. Someone brought in platters of food, someone else called our friends to check on Jay, I cleared off surfaces, located plates and flatware, and behaved like a woman in a highly efficient daze, which I was. At some point people started going home for the night, but none of us wanted my father to be in his house alone so Phillip and I insisted he stay with us. The place was in utter disarray and I was fretting about where to put him.

"Robin, darling," my father said. "Don't worry about setting up a bed for me. I'm not going to sleep. I'm just going to sit here on the couch." I left the living room thinking, *I can't go to bed and leave him here by himself.* Which was, of course, exactly what needed to happen. But I'm always worrying about everybody, even when they don't need me to.

The next morning I woke up and it hit me: my mother is gone. My next thought was to check on my father. I ran downstairs and there he was, sitting on the sofa. It looked as if he hadn't moved all night.

"How are you doing this morning, daddy?" I said.

"I'm going to be okay," he said. "Your mother came to me last night." I stared at him.

"What?"

"She came and sat right beside me last night and told me not to worry, that she was happy and she would see me again. And I promise you, I'm going to be okay."

I was flabbergasted. My father was the kind of man who, if you'd told him a week earlier that his wife was going to die and come to back to him to tell him that everything would be okay, would have said you were nuts. But there was such strength and peace in his voice, I felt hopeful that he would be alright.

Friends began to show up and even more relatives arrived, some of whom I hadn't seen in years and barely knew or recognized. I don't remember much about that time, but I do know it was horrible. We were still in shock and all these people were milling about in this dingy old house full of boxes, asking where the bathroom was (I barely knew myself) and trying to think of something nice to say. We would take turns driving to the hospital to see Grandma, then return to the house and deal with choosing a casket and making funeral arrangements.

I was in a state of emotional turmoil—efficient one moment, sobbing the next—and at some point Phillip took me aside and suggested we go talk to the minister at our church. It was the first time I'd ever lost anyone close, and Phillip wanted to make sure he was doing everything to help me. At that point, I was open to anything that might dull the ache in my heart, and it was a chance to get away from the hordes of people at the house.

We drove to the church and sat down with the minister, who said all the things he was supposed to say under the circumstances. He was trying to comfort me and I was grateful for his efforts, but what I remember most was a feeling of awe, because at that point, oddly enough, I wasn't as sad for myself as I was for my mother. The things he said were meant to ease my suffering, and they did; but I remember thinking, *What is wrong with me? I feel sorry for my loss but at the same time, I feel sorrier for hers.* My mother was such a precious woman; she loved her life and she was happy all the time, or at least she wanted you to think she was. All she wanted was for everyone to be happy. That's what was causing me the worst anguish, the thought that she had been denied the chance to live the life she loved so much.

After about fifteen minutes we thanked the minister and left. Perhaps my mother was in a better place, as he suggested; but I felt in my heart, perhaps selfishly, that there was no better place for my mother than right here on earth with her family. She had been cheated out of what was most precious to her—time with the people she loved—and we had been cheated out of time with her.

The combination of grief and busyness and relatives turned that time into a blur. But I do remember feeling, along with my siblings, an overriding anxiety about the funeral, which would take place the following day, and a creeping dread that my father would start drinking again. It had been about six years since my father joined AA and my mother returned to their marriage. But now, with her so suddenly and shockingly gone, we feared that my father would drown his pain in whisky. It was like being a little kid again and worrying, *Is he going to go out and get drunk again? Is this the night he's going to get himself killed or kill someone else?*

Later that day, a sort of miracle happened. My father gathered Karin, Cindi, Jamie, Roger, and me around him. "I know you kids are worried I'm going to drink again and I want you to know I won't do that," he said. "Your mother deserves better than that. I will not use her sudden, early death as a reason to drink. That would be an insult to her, and I would never do that."

You can know someone your whole life and he may still surprise you, and my father surprised me that day. No one is completely weak or completely strong, after all; most of us are both courageous and vulnerable, and sometimes it takes a crisis to reveal what we're made of. I had always perceived my father as weak because of all the years he wouldn't or couldn't stop drinking. I was accustomed to feeling pity for him, but because of the promise he had made, now I also felt respect.

I don't remember much about the funeral, other than that there were a lot of people at the service. And it wasn't until I sat down to write this book that I realized the reason I never visualize the burial is that I wasn't there. I remember arriving at the cemetery and everyone else leaving to go to the gravesite. But I didn't go with them because my father would not get out of the car and I didn't want to leave him behind. I must have sent them all ahead, including Phillip.

I remember getting back into the car and my father saying, "I don't think I can do this; I can't do this," and so I sat there with him. All that mattered to me at that point was to take care of my dad, so we both missed the burial. Looking back, it all makes sense: I'm happiest when I'm taking care of someone, and I felt no conflict about missing the burial. I knew that I was the only person who could comfort him. As we prayed together in the car, I knew that my mother would have wanted it to be that way. It was, quite simply, the right thing to do.

I replayed my mother's death over and over in my mind during the days that followed. First it made me cry, and then it made me think.

I was thirty-one years old, married for eight years, and the mother of a six-year-old boy. There was nothing in the world as precious to me as my husband and son. Just as my mother had always put her family's needs before her own, I had put my family's needs before mine. Like most mothers, I daydreamed about the milestones to come in Jay's life, and pictured myself beaming beside him as he grew stronger and taller and took his place in the world. In my mind I was always there, smiling and protecting him and making sure he was happy, just as my mother always did for us . . .

And then it would hit me. She was gone.

I was a mother and my own

> It was then that I realized that loving your family and neglecting yourself are not the same thing; that, in fact, if a woman truly loves her family, she must not and will not neglect herself.

mother was dead. My young son would grow up without his grandmother and perhaps forget what she looked like, or even that she existed. My life was immeasurably, profoundly diminished because she was gone. And she was gone because she didn't take care of herself.

It was then that I realized that loving your family and neglecting yourself are not the same thing; that, in fact, if a woman truly loves her family, she must not and will not neglect herself. It was the same kind of revelatory moment I had as a teenager, when I realized that my father was a drunk. This time, I realized that my mother had martyred herself for the sake of her family, and we were all the poorer for it.

When I thought of her baking that pie while she was having a heart attack, I felt as if my own heart would crack with grief. The thought of it sitting on the stove, cold and uneaten in that lonely house, hurt me so much I asked Phillip to drive over there before the funeral and throw it away. Under no circumstances could I bear to walk into that house and see it.

It seems strange when I think about it now: that pie was the last thing my mother touched. She made it out of love for me, and, had she delivered it to our new house that Sunday, I would have savored every bite as the token of love it was. Yet after she died, I could not bear the thought of even looking at it. Why? Why did it not seem even more precious after she was gone? Why did I not want to taste it and remember her wonderful baking? Why did I not choose to freeze it as people do a slice of their wedding cake, to preserve the memory of the love it signified?

The reason, I believe, is that the pie became for me a symbol of the colossal self-neglect that had taken my mother's life. I could not bear to look at it, let alone taste it, because it was the thing she was paying attention to when she should have been paying attention to herself.

I didn't understand. Why her? Why me, why us? Why now, with my father finally sober, and their marriage better than it had perhaps ever been? Why hadn't I seen this coming? I was so intuitive, so perceptive; how could I not have seen that my mother needed rest, care, help? How could I have been so blind? Maybe if I had let her come over that morning as she'd offered to do, I might have been able to save her.

As I keep saying, I like to exercise control over my life, and I'm pretty good at it. But my mother's death and other losses since then have taught me that no matter how organized and vigilant we are, from time to time life still has a way of bringing us to our knees. Like it or not, there are some things that cannot be controlled; not by me, not by anyone. Innocent children get hurt, hardworking adults lose their pensions, cities are blown away by hurricanes, and beloved wives, mothers, and grandmothers collapse and die of heart attacks while baking pies for their daughters. You can lament and carry on all you want to, but bad stuff happens to good people and there's not much any of us can do about it except choose how to respond. That is all any of us can do. And ultimately, it's all that matters.

I got my first inkling of this fairly early in my marriage. Phillip had this one relative I couldn't figure out. One day this person would act as if I were the best thing that had ever happened to the family, the next, as if I were an evil person who didn't deserve to live. It was confusing because I grew up wanting everyone to get along; when you live with an alcoholic parent, the *last* thing you want to do is create conflict. So at family gatherings I'd come in all cheery and friendly and everything would be fine until the two of us would end up alone in a room together and this person would make a critical remark and leave me standing there, stung and reeling with confusion.

I took it very personally. Why was this person treating me this way? I wasn't about to make a scene; this was Phillip's family and I was the newest part of it. It was my job to be sweet, and (the way I saw it) it was Phillip's job to manage his family and make them treat me properly. So I would tell Phillip about these episodes and wait for him to say, "Robin, you are the kindest, most loving person on the planet, and no one has the right to treat you this way. I'm going to go over and straighten things out once and for all."

But he never said that. What he consistently said was, "You know what? This person did have the right to say that." And man, every time he said it, it felt like he'd slapped me. I felt like saying, "Now, wait a minute, buddy—you're supposed to be on my side!"

And he would look at me in this levelheaded way and say, "No, Robin. You're not going to convince me otherwise. This person had the right to say it. *But you have the right not to react to it.*" Every time Phillip said it I'd get mad at him, and I was mad a lot because this went on for a while. Whenever I went to Phillip for comfort, he'd say, "No, they had every right to say that," which drove me wild because I thought he was telling me that he agreed with this person. But the essence of what he was telling me, every time, was,

You can't control other people. You cannot control what they say, what they think, or what they do. People have the right to think and say whatever they want to. But you have the right not to take it to heart, and not to react.

"When you allow a person's words to upset you, you're giving away your power," he said (in one of his early personal appearances as Dr. Phil). "You are giving someone else the power to control how you feel and how you think. You need to say, 'You have the right to say it and you have the right to think it. But I have the right to disagree: I have the right to not react; I have the right to continue to believe what I know is true.'"

I didn't like hearing it, but Phillip kept repeating it until one day a light bulb went on in my head and I realized, *He is neither betraying me nor agreeing with his relative; in fact, he completely disagrees. The reason he has this calmness about him is because he is dismissing this person's comments as nonsense, and he thinks I should do the same.*

He was right. And from that day forward, I have always known that what other people think of me or say about me ought not to influence what I know to be true about myself. To doubt myself because of others would be to hand over my power to them, and that is something I will not do. I never give my power away.

> *You can't control other people. You cannot control what they say, what they think, or what they do. People have the right to think and say whatever they want to. But you have the right not to take it to heart, and not to react.*

That's exactly what you do when you allow someone else's opinion of you to affect your opinion of yourself: you're giving away your power. And I say, don't do it. It doesn't matter how convinced of your flaws your detractors may be; if you allow other people to erode your good opinion of yourself, you're giving them power over you. This family member truly felt righteous about judging me harshly, but what I failed to see at the time was that the judgment was more about that person than it was about me. Some combination of irrational thoughts, distorted perceptions, and unknowable events in that person's life motivated those behaviors. Ultimately (and ironically), it had nothing to do with me. The moment I accepted this person's right to be conflicted and in turmoil, I was able to restore my own equanimity. I now enjoy a warm relationship with this person because I made a decision—just as I did with my father—to allow in only the positive aspects of the relationship and to reject the bad ones. I could not control this person, but I could control myself.

This lesson came into play a few years later when my mother died. I realized that it was too late to persuade her to take better care of herself, but it wasn't too late for me to learn from her tragedy and vow to take care of myself.

And I do. Ever since my mother died, I take care of myself as if my life depended on it. I do a breast self-exam in the shower several times a month. I go to the dentist every six months and have my teeth cleaned and checked. Every year I get a complete physical, a mammogram, and a Pap smear. And pardon me if I get on a soapbox here, ladies, but I'm talking to you. If you have not seen a doctor in the last year, please, please take a moment to think about yourself, about the gift of life that God has given you, and how little it takes for you to protect that gift. If you're not convinced, think about the people who love you—your husband, your children, your parents—and think about what their lives would be like without you. That's precisely the process I went through when my mother died: I pictured Jay having to grow up without me and Phillip having to raise him without me. I vowed I would always, always take care of myself—if not for my sake, then for theirs.

I am only six years younger than my mother was when she died. I've done the math, and according to my calculations (and by the grace of God), I believe I have thirty to forty years left. I have two sons to marry off, richly imagined grandchildren to love and spoil, a husband to love and spoil, important work to do through the Dr. Phil Foundation, and who knows what kinds of career opportunities yet to pursue. As I see it, there is no excuse for me to do less than everything I can to be the best that I can be for a long, long time.

So I do everything I can, and, what I can't do, my doctor does. I have blood work done and my hormone levels checked regularly. I've had a full-body scan—a noninvasive, painless procedure where a machine scans your body to see if anything is growing where it shouldn't be—and a bone density scan, which checks for signs of osteoporosis (women are especially vulnerable to osteoporosis if they have small bones or have given birth). I had a colonoscopy when I turned forty-five and I'll have another one in the next few years: if you catch colon cancer early it's easy to cure, but if you wait long enough to have symptoms, it can be deadly. I have also had a heart scan, which checks to see if your arteries are clear, and I have my cholesterol levels checked regularly.

I am careful to take care of my heart, because coronary disease runs in my family. Nobody knows this better than my brother, Roger. Not long before we moved to Los Angeles, Roger stopped by for a visit and started having chest pain. Phillip put Roger in the car and took him to the doctor. Roger did a stress test and it came out normal, but the doctor happened to be a cardiologist and said he wanted to do some blood tests to be on the safe side. Roger rolled up his sleeve and ten minutes later the doctor came back to say that Roger's enzyme levels were so bad that he was scheduling my brother for an angiogram the next day. It turned out that one of Roger's arteries was over 95 percent blocked; two days later, he had triple bypass surgery.

So I have my blood enzymes checked, along with a lot of other things. And it's not as if I abused my body before my mother died; in fact, I've always loved to exercise. But the day my mother died was when I made a conscious choice to maintain my body for health reasons, not just so I would look good. I am neither a hypochondriac nor one of those people who freaks out if she doesn't exercise for three hours every day. But I have made it my business to learn about my genetics and conditions to which I may be predisposed. My mother died of heart disease and my father died of cancer, so those are two conditions I need to watch out for.

This goes for everyone: you have to learn your family's medical history to get a sense of the future of your own health. If your mother and her sister have both suffered from breast cancer, your odds of getting it may be higher than those of a woman whose family has no history of the disease. If your grandfather died of colon cancer it doesn't mean you're going to get it, but it does mean you should tell your doctor about it and ask when he or she thinks you should have a colonoscopy. (For the record, a colonoscopy is no big deal. If you're over fifty and haven't had one done because you're too squeamish to deal with it, stop acting like a baby and go have one. This is your life we're talking about.)

You have to learn about your family's medical history (and your spouse's) not only for your own sake but for the sake of your children. You'd be amazed at how many medical conditions are hereditary: diabetes, Crohn's disease, certain auto-immune disorders, heart illness, depression, anxiety disorders, and hundreds of other problems can be genetically linked. So not only do I feel I need to know about my own health; I need to know about the well-being of my husband and my children, too. Because if they are suffering in any way, physically or emotionally, I am going to do whatever it takes to make it better. I go on the Internet, rev up my favorite search engines, and read everything I can get my eyes on.

I also do whatever it takes to make myself feel better. When I was in my mid-forties, I started having hot flashes and went to see my gynecologist. I explained how I was feeling and she took some blood, saying she wanted to see me again the following week to go over the results.

When I returned, she entered the office with a grim look on her face. I was scared to death; what was wrong with me? She sat down at her desk, opened my file, and gave me the bad news.

"Robin, life as you know it is over—you're in menopause." She shook her head sadly as if to say, "Oh, you poor thing."

I was shocked. Menopause is a natural part of life that every woman will experience; why was she treating it like a tragedy? Admittedly, I didn't know much about the menopausal transition—yet—so I felt a bit overwhelmed and anxious at first. Still, it seemed to me that this part of my life didn't have to have such tragic overtones. The next thing I knew, she was handing me a stack of prescriptions.

"Fill these as soon as you leave here and get started on them right away," she said.

"What are these?" I asked.

"Synthetic hormones. Trust me, you're going to need them." I looked through the slips of paper and tried to make out her handwriting—estrogen, progesterone, testosterone, DHEA, an antidepressant. I was floored.

"Do you give these to all your patients?"

"All of them going through menopause."

Now, I'm not a doctor, but it seemed odd to me that every menopausal patient would need precisely the same medications. I said so, and it seemed to hit a nerve.

"Trust me on this. You have no idea what you're in for." *Not yet*, I thought, *but I will by this time tomorrow.*

"You know," I said, "I'd really prefer to do this more naturally. I go to an acupuncturist and see a homeopathic practitioner, and I think I'd like to visit with both of them before I start any prescription drugs."

She looked at me with real pity this time. "Look, Robin," she said, "if you don't take those drugs, you'll be back here in three months begging me to help you."
And I thought, *Lady, I'm not the begging type.* I thanked her for her time and stuffed the prescriptions in my purse. I may have walked in a woman in menopause, but I walked out a woman on a mission.

That day, I made a choice to turn that time of my life into a positive event, and because of that choice, I

> That day, I took charge of my health and made it my business to know my body and what it needed to thrive—and I urge every woman to do the same.

believe today I am the healthiest I've ever been. That day, I took charge of my health and made it my business to know my body and what it needed to thrive—and I urge every woman to do the same. And don't wait until you're middle-aged—the sooner you start taking care of yourself, the better your chances are of enjoying robust health as you age. And if you're already in midlife, start now—it's never, ever too late to get healthier.

To this day, when there's a health issue I want to learn about, I go straight to the bookstore, sit on the floor, skim every book on the subject, and buy the ones I want to read. I shop in health food stores (you can learn a lot from the people who work there), talk with pharmacists (they know a lot about not only medications but also the doctors who prescribe them), and I read every magazine, newsletter, pamphlet, and periodical I can get my hands on that can help me keep myself and my loved ones healthy.

I don't do this because I think I can control everything; I do it because I know I cannot. I know so many women who never look after themselves because they think it would be selfish to spend money on going to the doctor or taking some time to relax. But I disagree; I believe a woman who takes care of herself *is* being a good wife and mother, because she's increasing her chances of staying alive and healthy to take care of the people she loves.

> I believe a woman who takes care of herself *is* being a good wife and mother, because she's increasing her chances of staying alive and healthy to take care of the people she loves.

My mother's death taught me that. After she died, my initial feeling of helplessness gave way to a sense of my personal power. I came to see that within every event lies a realm of possible responses, and by choosing among them I would define who I was. And I'm not talking only about grand, life-changing events; I'm talking about everyday happenings and interactions, like the ones you get into with the people you love and live with, and the one I got into with my husband.

In the days and weeks after the funeral, many people reached out to me. They brought food, they brought flowers, they called, they sent cards; most of all, they reminded me that even though my mother was gone I was far from alone in the world, and it touched me deeply. When my mother was buried and everyone went home,

I told Phillip that it was important for me to sit down and write thank-you notes to everyone who had come to honor my mother's memory. I wanted to let them know how much their affection meant to me, and I wanted to do it while the feelings were still fresh. And Phillip said, "Absolutely."

I went to the store, bought boxes and boxes of cream-colored stationery, and set myself up on the dining room table. For four days I sat in that dreary, musty room writing notes and letters, every one by hand. I thanked people for reaching out to me and then would cry and sob as I wrote about my mother and told them about how wonderful she was. I'd get Jay up and off to school, send Phillip off to work, and then sit there all day, stopping only to cook dinner and tuck Jay into bed. It was a therapeutic experience for me because I got to think about my mother in the context of all these people she had known. It gave me a chance to think about her not only as my mother but as a friend, neighbor, relative, and colleague of many other people, all of whom had known her in a different way than I had. I would sit there until I was all cried out; then I'd go to bed and start again the next morning.

I finally finished the notes. I put a stamp on each one, stacked them up, put them in a little bag, handed them to Phillip, and said, "If you'll mail these for me tomorrow at the office, I can now start living my life without my mother." And he took the bag and said, "Of course I will."

My pain at losing my mother was so enormous, so overwhelming, I felt I had to set some limits so it wouldn't take over my life. So I gave myself permission to grieve while I wrote those notes, literally to my heart's content. I told myself that I would get through the pain by feeling it with every stroke of my pen; then, when I was done writing about my mother, it would be time to start living without her. It was tough; there were days when I'd break down and cry every ten minutes, but I was committed to moving forward each day without her, because that's what she would have wanted. And that's what I did.

One morning about three weeks later while Phillip was in the shower, I picked up his tennis bag and swung it onto the bed. Phillip was in private practice at the time, and at the end of the day he would stop and play tennis before coming home. I would typically get the bag ready for him and put in his tennis shoes, tennis shorts, clean socks, and a T-shirt, and he'd take it to work with him. I realized that I hadn't done it in a while and felt like getting back into my old routine.

I gathered up his tennis clothes and was putting them into the bag when I felt something bulging in from a side pocket. And I thought, *Ugh, I bet that sweaty shirt has been in there since the last time I emptied this thing.* I unzipped the pocket and reached down in there, and what did I find but the bag full of thank-you notes.

My heart broke. It was as if my mother had died all over again.

I started crying. And as I stood there weeping and missing my mother, Phillip walked into the room. He stared at me and he stared at those notes and he stood there with the most horrified look on his face.

"Oh . . . my . . . God," he said, his voice barely a whisper. "I forgot to mail them." I was really sobbing now.

"I thought they knew! I thought they knew! I've seen these people, Phillip, in the store, and on the street, and I never said a word of thanks to them because I thought they'd gotten my cards! I thought they knew!" The poor man just stood there. His face was the color of ashes.

I was hurt, I was angry, I was in pieces all over again. Not only had I felt good about thanking so many people for comforting me, but writing to them about my mother and imagining them reading what I'd written was a huge part of my healing process. I had seen these people around town, and it had given me comfort to know that there had been an exchange between us, that I had properly acknowledged their condolences, expressed my gratitude for their caring, and left them knowing a little bit more about my mother after her death than they had known when she was alive.

I think it's important to let people know when they have comforted you. At a time when I felt constantly pricked by sharp reminders of my loss, these good people had provided me with compassion and friendship that cushioned my heart. At the time, I felt I was repaying their kindness by writing, with my own hand, anecdotes about what a wonderful woman my mother had been. Then when I'd see these people in town I would imagine we shared a bond and think, *We are some of the lucky ones, you and I, because we share this secret of how extraordinary my mother was, and how great a loss it is that she is gone.*

But now that illusion was also gone; there was no knowledge between us, no secret shared. I felt like one of those palm trees you see on Weather Channel hurricane updates, blasted about by gale-force emotional winds that could blow me over at any moment. I felt devastated and shocked and sad and angry.

I also felt betrayed: *Here I believed you thought it was important for me to sit and write these notes—you told me you did—so how could you forget?* That was the crux of it: how could this matter so little to him? How could this man think he knew me and not realize the value of these notes? How could he think he loved me if he couldn't remember to do this one hugely important thing?

I looked up and Phillip was standing in the same place quietly saying, "I'll cancel my patients and I'll spend the whole day . . . I'll call them . . . I'll make a list and call them. I'll get their phone numbers, I'll call everyone—no, I'll go see them, that's what I'll do, I'll hand-deliver the notes. Just give them to me and I'll go right now, Robin, I'll do whatever it takes. Please, please let me make this up to you."

And something melted inside me and I thought, *Bless his heart.* This precious man is devastated, just as I am, and suddenly I knew that his feelings were more important to me than the feelings of the people who hadn't received the notes. I thought, *He is suffering so much more for not mailing the notes than they are for not receiving them; what do I gain by punishing him with my anger? What benefit do I derive by making him suffer more?*

This was a powerful moment for me personally and a pivotal one in our marriage. At that moment, I had the opportunity to show this man who I really was, this man who had told me years ago, "People have the right to think and say and do whatever they want to. And you have the right to choose not to react."

I had the right to rant and rave and scream and yell and make Phillip feel horrible. *I had the right to behave that way, but that's not who I am.* Instead, I seized the opportunity to show him who I actually was: a compassionate and forgiving woman who loved him, no matter what, and who would forgive him, no matter what.

So I looked into his sad, sad eyes and blotted my own with my sleeve. "I know you didn't do it on purpose," I said. "We'll mail them today and they'll get them tomorrow. I love you and I know you love me, and I know you didn't do it on purpose." And the look of gratitude on his face showed me how fortunate he felt. I think of that moment as the one when Phillip learned that my love for him and commitment to him were stronger than any mistake he might make. I believe that was the moment he learned he could trust me, and he has never forgotten it.

Nor have I forgotten what I learned that day about the nature of love and mercy and forgiveness and their role in a working marriage. Phillip clearly felt compassion for me, so I was able to feel compassion for him. Believe me, if he had found

> Every day offers a chance to choose either anger or understanding, bitterness or acceptance, darkness or light. And the choices we make reveal the stuff we're made of.

me crying over his tennis bag and said, "What's the big deal? Just give them to me and I'll mail them today—" Whoa! I'd be a lot less forthcoming in the compassion department. But he didn't measure my reaction against the yardstick of his emotions because he knew—and knows—that I am not him. We neither think alike nor feel alike, and the depth of our love for each other lies in mutual acceptance, not denial, of our differences.

How could Phillip have forgotten to mail those notes? The answer is simple: He forgot because they weren't nearly as important to him as they were to me, and they didn't weigh as much on his heart and mind as they did on mine. There's no way they could have: Phillip has many ways of expressing gratitude, but writing thank-you notes isn't his first choice.

Which is precisely the point. That parcel of envelopes was, for Phillip, a parcel of envelopes. It was not for him what it was for me: a precious collection of reminiscences about my mother, destined to be shared with people who had honored her memory and touched me in the process. His failure to mail them was evidence of neither a lack of love for me nor respect for my way of grieving. He had merely forgotten to run an errand, and he deserved to be forgiven for that.

I believe in forgiveness. I believe that, just as God promises to forgive us, He wants us to forgive one another. Every day offers a chance to choose either anger or understanding, bitterness or acceptance, darkness or light. And the choices we make reveal the stuff we're made of. In the darkness that engulfed me when I lost my mother, I chose to light a candle when I vowed not to neglect myself as she had. And on those rare occasions when Phillip and I have a disagreement, I try to remind myself that an argument is really an opportunity to show my husband who I am. And believe me, I use all of those opportunities. It is an option every woman has, if only she will use it. It's your choice.

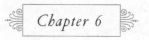

Chapter 6

A WIFE'S HEART

Choosing to Do Whatever Makes
My Husband Happy

I am in the audience at the *Dr. Phil* show every day, and I have
been since it first aired four years ago. I absolutely love it; I
wouldn't miss it for the world.

I love being there because this show—the work my husband
does in that time—is his life's passion. It is his calling and he has
asked me to be there with him and for him. I love that he wants
me there and I love that I can be there. Yes, there are plenty of
other things I could do with my time, but none of them means
more to me than being in the studio because I share Phillip's passion for this important work. I absolutely love watching him
work. He loves doing the show, and few things make me happier
than watching him do what he loves to do. Over the last few
years I have been able to contribute in small ways. Let's face it:

Dr. Phil could do with some fine-tuning of his feminine side now and again.

The *Dr. Phil* show isn't just Phillip's job; it's part of the fabric of our lives. It's the reason we decided to exchange the down-home familiarity of our old Texas existence for the comparatively fast-paced surroundings of our new one, and we negotiated the move the same way we did every other evolution in our marriage.

It's not every day your husband gets a chance to star in his own television show. And while I believed that doing the *Dr. Phil* show was a terrific opportunity for my husband, I also knew that there were other people to consider, especially Jordan. He was fifteen when the show became a real possibility and we knew that relocating from Dallas to Los Angeles would require a major adjustment on his part—one that might be difficult for a teenager to make. Jay had just graduated from college and was preparing to enter law school, so he was already on his own. But Jordan was still living with us and was part of a network of friendships and activities that he would have to abandon if we moved.

Phillip and I sat down and considered our options, which included saying no to the show and staying in Dallas; saying yes and moving the family to Los Angeles; or saying yes and having Phillip move to Los Angeles while Jordan and I stayed behind. Splitting up the family was out of the question, which left doing the show and moving, or turning it down and staying where we were. As much as Phillip wanted to do the show, we both agreed that this was a clear-cut case of putting family first; so we sat down with Jordan and said we were not about to make the move unless he convinced us he was behind it. It turned out that Jordan liked the idea of living in Los Angeles; he knew he would have some adjusting to do, but then, so would we all. This way, we could do it together.

We were all hugely psyched about moving to California, so you can imagine my surprise when I realized that not everyone was as gung-ho as we were. "Oh, your lives will be an open book now," many people said. "Everyone will know you and it will change who you are; you'll become cold and hard and bitter—you'll see." I was shocked at how many people had a negative attitude about this adventure on which we were about to embark. And I thought, *No—no one, not one thing will ever change what we've created in our lives.* And I'm pleased to say that, four years later, we are still exactly who we were the day we moved out here, and that's because it was a choice we made.

Now, you may be wondering how a family could relocate from a life of relative obscurity in Dallas to one of tour-bus visibility in Los Angeles and not change. And the fact is, many things around us have changed. Phillip goes to work on a soundstage instead of an office, and for the first time, I go with him. We live in a house fortified to withstand earthquakes instead of tornadoes, and we seldom have to come up with alternate plans in case it rains.

Our California house feels very different inside than our home in Texas: this one is done in Italian Renaissance style, with dark wooden built-in bookshelves and cabinets; the other one was French Mediterranean, with a brighter, more casual feel. But I designed and decorated them both, from floor (mosaic) to ceiling (vaulted); and as different as they are, they both reflect me and they both feel like home. (They apparently both smell like home, or at least Phillip says so.)

Another reason this house feels different is that Jordan doesn't live here anymore. It's quieter at night than it used to be, and sometimes I miss the heartwarming, earsplitting racket that a boy and his guitar can make. On the other hand, I don't feel obligated to cook dinner every night, so Phillip and I eat a lot of take-out meals, and I'm not complaining (for the record, neither is he). So, yes, some outward aspects of our lives are different than they used to be. But the essence of our family and the core of our marriage remain constant no matter where we live or what we do: no one and nothing is ever going to change who we are.

Not that the tabloids haven't tried. To read some of the things that have been written, you would think we had undergone some sort of personality replacement procedure on the way out here. I can't tell you where some of these people get their ideas from—I suspect it's a conference room of harried reporters reduced to creating faux news—but I can tell you that more than 90 percent of every story about us that has appeared in the tabloids or trash books is ridiculous fiction.

One day our publicist came in to brief us on stories about us that would soon be appearing in the press. We usually have an idea about the fantasy of the week, but we don't comment on the stories, and in fact we don't read them anymore. At first they were bothersome but it doesn't take long to get a pretty thick skin. So anyway, one day our publicist comes in and says, "Robin, a story is coming out next week that says you hate it out here and that you're bored and lonely because you miss your bunco league, and that you wish you could have a baby girl."

I looked at him and said, "Oh my gosh, I could do for a precious little girl (occasionally) but I absolutely love it out here. And what in the world is bunco? And whatever it is, please tell me Champagne is involved." We looked it up on the Internet and learned that bunco is a sort of dice game dating back to the 1850s. (Champagne is optional.) It sounded like fun, but I had never even heard of it, let alone played it.

Sure enough, this preposterous story appeared in the paper, describing me as out of my element and in need of friends, wandering the streets of Beverly Hills, going door to door like a hungry dog and saying, "Hello, do you bunco? Do you bunco?" And the story actually said that women would come to their doors and look at me as if to say, "Oh, you silly little Texas girl! This is Beverly Hills—we don't play bunco here."

Whatever. When you live in the public eye, you have to learn to roll with the punches. And I learned to do just that by following some good advice from my dear friend Oprah.

Something these papers regularly do is print stories about how Dr. Phil is bitterly feuding with Oprah. Now, you will never meet a woman sweeter than Oprah Winfrey, and they have never had a cross word. She is so proud of us both. She is kind and abundantly generous in every sense of the word.

It was Oprah, after all, who first invited Phillip to appear on national television (they met in the mid-1990s when she was sued by some Texas cattlemen and her lawyers hired Phillip's company to help them prepare for the trial, which she won), and it was her idea that Phillip should have his own show. And it is a measure of her character that, when Phillip was offered his own show and it became clear we would be moving out west, that she reacted like a mother when her kids go off to college, always staying in touch.

I remember her calling when we first got here, asking how I was doing. Next week, same deal. "How are you? Do you need anything? How's it going?" Thankfully, she has nothing to worry about: I thrive on change, and Phillip and I love it out here. But that just shows how sweet Oprah is, and how upsetting it is when a story comes out pitting Phillip against this woman who is his partner, champion, and one of my dearest friends.

I remember one of these feuding stories coming out not long after we got here, and I called Oprah up to tell her how bad we felt that people were being misled into thinking Phillip and she were fighting. And she said to me, "Robin, this is what they do. They sit around the table on Monday morning and they say, 'Okay, what can we write about this week? What's hot?'" And she explained that if there isn't some real gossip—say, some hunky movie star running around with his nanny, or some skin-and-bones starlet showing that in nine months or so she's going to *need* a nanny—they'll say, "There's nothing really happening right now . . . so, who's hot? Who can we write about?" And they'll start throwing out names and create their own stories.

Which they do, with occasionally hilarious results. Phillip's favorite was an investigative piece on how Dr. Phil and Robin could be married for thirty years and still be happy after moving to

Hollywood, the divorce capital of the world. And the answer was that he writes me love songs and sings them to me while perching on the edge of our bathtub (as I'm soaking in it, I suppose). Now I ask you, how would anyone know what we're doing in our bathroom? Yet the story was confirmed by "sources close to Robin and Dr. Phil." One of the first lessons we learned after moving to Los Angeles was that when "sources" confirm a story rather than real people with real names, it means the story is made up.

But you know what? The adventure we're having here more than makes up for the adjustments we've had to make. I love change—we've never lived in a house for more than five years—and I'm thriving on the changes we've made since coming here.

Producing a daily television series is not like a normal job, where you put in your time, go home, and forget about work until you go back the next day. With the possible exception of when he's asleep, Phillip is always thinking about the show, whether it's the theme of the next day's program or the guests he'll be working with or possible ways to address the problems they're having.

The people who come on the show are real, their problems are real, and they've been coping with them for years or perhaps their whole lives before they sit down with Dr. Phil. Their appearances are not rehearsed, so whatever transpires is completely spontaneous.

That said, he is well prepared for the encounter. He does his homework! Phillip works closely with the producers to decide which topics to deal with, which guests to include, and what focus he wants each show to have. He studies videotapes of the guests along with a thick notebook compiled by his staff containing extensive personal and family interviews with the guests and a wealth of developmental background information.

The night before taping, Phillip settles into his study for four or five hours with the notebook and the videotapes until he is comfortable with the dynamics of the guests. He frequently consults with a distinguished group of experts from the nation's leading universities and treatment centers, which comprise the *Dr. Phil* show advisory board. I typically join him in the study while he prepares, and I love being a sounding board, especially regarding the female point of view. By the end of the night, he understands the problems the next day's guests are facing, and how he plans to approach them, but it isn't until he meets and converses with them onstage that he gets a more complete sense of who they are and how he can best help them.

Phillip will be the first one to tell you that his goal on the show is education, not therapy. Obviously, you can't do psychotherapy in twenty minutes, while breaking for commercials, no less. His hope is that every day people will tune in, see a guest with a problem they can relate to, and maybe get some ideas about how they might deal with it better in their own life. That's the beauty of the show: the people watching at home can get as much or more out of it than the guests do.

I have great respect for people who come on the show. I think they are courageous, inspirational, and dedicated to learning how to live a better life. They end up helping not only themselves but a lot of other people as well. Phillip and I both believe that the show is among those that embody the highest and best use of television.

He is delivering commonsense information to people's homes every day, free of charge. He never expects people to substitute his judgment for their own, but he does want to make them think. It warms my heart to read the thousands and thousands of letters we receive every month about the changes people are making in their lives because of the show.

When Phillip does a show on parenting, for example, we get letters from parents saying things such as, "Until I saw that show, I never realized what I was doing to my children. God bless you for a much-needed wakeup call." I feel really good inside because I know that maybe, just maybe, a small child will get a hug and a kiss that night instead of cruelty and pain. I know that everything Phillip has done in his life up until now was designed to prepare him for this moment.

And after four years of broadcasts, I continue to be amazed at how skilled and passionate his staff is at creating meaningful television. The people who end up on that stage are clearly supposed to be there, and as different as their stories are, the one thing they have in common is that they all want a better life.

I love to be there every day, and I'm beginning to get used to the camera homing in on me when Phillip decides he wants to ask me something during a taping. You know, like when he's got on a husband who calls his wife nasty names and Phillip says, "Well, I've gotta tell you, if I ever spoke to my wife that way—and I never have, never will—but if I ever did, I'd do it exactly once, because she'd never let me do it a second time." And suddenly there I am, filling up the screen, nodding as if to say, *You've got that right, buddy*. That's why I'm always wearing a microphone, because if Phillip asks me something, no one will hear my answer unless I'm miked. I know I'm not an expert about anything except my own experience, but if I can contribute to a show, I love being a part of it.

I also think my presence is valuable in that most of the people who watch my husband are women, and a lot of his shows deal with women's issues, so I can be his "friend at the factory." Sure, he's lived with a menopausal woman—that would be me—but there are certain times when he just needs a good dose of a woman's perspective!

Sometimes while walking over to the soundstage, he'll turn to me and say, "I'm coming to you today when we're talking about father-daughter relationships, okay?" The first time he said that I got all flustered and was stuttering, "What? What do you mean? What am I supposed to say?" Phillip told me to speak honestly and from the heart, which is what I did. I'm more comfortable with it now than I was four years ago when we started, but even so, it's intimidating when you know the camera is on and the whole world is watching.

I always think, *Oh, my gosh, I don't want to sound stupid. I don't want to offend anyone.* But in the end I still say just what I really feel and believe. And sometimes I don't have time to worry about sounding stupid because Phillip doesn't warn me at all. Sometimes he'll just turn to me from the stage and say, "This is Robin, and she knows a lot about this particular issue," and suddenly the camera is on my face and my face is on your TV screen, big as all get-out.

And let me tell you, it takes some getting used to: things always look bigger on camera than they actually are. Take hair. I spent the whole first season trying to get rid of the Texas hair look. I have so much hair that a good cut will last me only three weeks; if I wait any longer than that I've got big hair going on all over again. I don't tease it or fluff it; it just does its thing. Even now, if I'm due for a haircut and I end up on camera, all I will see is this itty-bitty face in the middle of all this hair.

Which I do myself, by the way, at home every morning, on big Velcro rollers because it's too heavy to hold a curl from a curling iron. I also do my own makeup, although if I know that we're taping an *Ask Dr. Phil and Robin* show that day, I'll let Tina or Mimi, Phillip's makeup and hair stylist, touch me up. They say I do a good job on my own but the camera is tricky; something that looks fine in real life can look terrible on camera, and these women are experts at knowing the difference.

That's why television shows have experts to deal with makeup, hair, and wardrobe: they know how to take people who look normal off-camera and adjust their appearance so they look normal on-camera—and no one looks normal on-camera unless someone puts a lot of work into it. Phillip has a closet full of suits at home that look terrific when he wears them out to dinner or to church but would not work for the show because either the cut or the fabric (or both) would not look good on camera. All the suits Phillip wears on television are made especially for that purpose, and they are kept at the studio where Becca, his wardrobe stylist, tends to them. She makes sure everything is altered, clean, pressed, and ready for Phillip to wear before he goes on stage.

That's one thing about Phillip: when it comes to his wardrobe, as long as he looks appropriate, he could not care less what he wears. His taste is all in his mouth, and he's always relied on me to dress him. Years ago when he'd travel on business and I'd have to stay behind with the boys, I'd pick out his clothes and pack them so he'd know what to wear with what. For instance, when he would fly to Chicago on Monday nights to be on *Oprah* the next day, I would pick out a suit, shirt, and tie, put them together, and tie a ribbon around them so he'd know to wear them together. If he needed more than one outfit, I would place each one in its own suit bag with matching belt and socks in the pocket. I'd even label his shoes "Day One" and "Day Two," leaving as little as possible to chance.

I remember one time Phillip was traveling somewhere to give a speech. I was going with him, so I packed all his clothes together in the suitcase, figuring I'd lay them out for him at the hotel. But within a few hours of arriving I got very sick with the flu and went to bed. He didn't want to wake me the next morning so he dressed himself and left to give his talk. I woke up midmorning and thought, *Oh my gosh, what did he wear?* I ran to the closet and—don't you know—he picked the wrong shirt and tie and wore them with the wrong suit! He had two to choose from—and he picked the wrong ones. (I think he got the shoes right, but now that I think about it, there may have been only one pair.)

Now, there are some men who are very particular about what they wear, and insist on picking out all their own clothes. If Phillip were like that, I'd be fine with it. But he isn't like that and never has been, so why shouldn't I do it for him? I love the way he looks when he's dressed up, and I love helping him look that way. I think the success of a marriage is in large part based on the willingness of each partner to do what it takes to meet the other's needs. And in my experience, men are pretty obvious about letting you know what they need; we women just have to learn to read the signals.

Men are different from us; they're not going to take us by the hand and say, "Sweetheart, I want to talk to you about these feelings I've been having," and beg us to do this, that, or the other thing—forget that. What they are going to do is get out of the shower twenty minutes before you're due to be somewhere and say, "So, what are you thinking of wearing tonight?" It doesn't matter that your outfit is laid out on the bed alongside seven others you've already rejected and they're all long, dressy, and black. Because he's not really asking you what you're going to wear, he's asking you to tell him what *he's* going to wear. It's a guy code they use to let us know that they need help without actually asking for it. That way, they get their needs met without having to admit to us that they actually have needs in the first place.

> I think the success of a marriage is in large part based on the willingness of each partner to do what it takes to meet the other's needs.

But men do have needs, of course, and all things considered, they're pretty good about putting the information out there for us to find. Which is why I'm astonished at the number of women who either don't pick up the signals their men are sending out or, even worse, pick them up loud and clear and choose to ignore them, as though it would diminish their power to help out.

I once knew a woman who was always at odds with her husband. They didn't argue or yell, but it was as if she had a constant, underlying need to get him before he got her. I couldn't figure it out; I never heard him speak unkindly or disrespectfully to her, and he seemed like a very decent man. Still, his happiness was never very high on her list of priorities.

I remember she was at the house once when her husband was away on a fishing trip and she was talking about how he loved to meet up with these old friends every year, and they would rent a boat and spend a week hanging out and being guys together. She said he'd been gone a week and was coming home that afternoon. I looked at the clock and saw that it was past three o'clock.

"You'd better get going," I said, "or you won't be there when he gets back."

"Oh, that's okay," she said.

"But don't you want to be there when he gets home?"

"No, not really."

"What?"

"Sure, he'd like me to be sitting there when he gets home so he can drag in his cooler and show me all the fish he caught. If he's so interested in being with me, why does he need to go away? If he's going to go away for a week, fine, but I'm sure as heck not going to be sitting there when he walks in, because that's exactly what he wants."

Was she kidding me? He's telling her what he wants, what he needs, what he likes, and she's not going to do it *on purpose*?

What's up with that?

If your mate lets you know what he wants and you use that information to hurt him, you've got to ask yourself why you are in the relationship in the first place. Here's this woman doing the opposite of what her husband wants so he won't think he can control her, whereas if she would wait for him to come home, crawl up in his lap and flirt with him, she'd have him hooked better than anything in that cooler of his. If I'd had my wits about me I'd have asked her how that was working for her, but I just sat there thinking, *Whoa—if my husband told me exactly what it would take to make him happy and I didn't use that information, how stupid would that be?* (Answer: *Very.*)

My being in the audience every day is a good example, because my being there makes my husband happy, and it would make no sense for me to be anywhere else—especially since Phillip makes no secret of his feelings on the subject. I've lost track of the times he's had on a couple heading for divorce, and he'll ask the husband if it's important that his wife feel proud of him. The husband, always, *always* says yes. No matter how viciously the couple argues and how little affection they show for each other, the husband always admits that he's hurt because his wife doesn't respect him and what he does for her and their family.

And then Phillip will say, "You know, I've got millions of people watching and thinking I'm doing a good job, and that's all well and good. But I've got to tell you that y'all's opinion doesn't mean a thing to me unless she—" and he nods toward me, "is proud of me and thinks I'm doing a good job. That's all I care about."

And the camera zooms in on my face, and I'm sitting there with tears in my eyes because I know it's true. I know that if I weren't proud of Phillip and if I didn't think he was doing good work, nothing we have would mean anything to him. And so, knowing how important it is to him that I hold him in high esteem, what better place is there for me to be than right there in the studio, watching him work and letting him know how proud I am of him?

You don't have to be a mind reader to figure out what your man wants and needs to be happy; he'll lay it out right there. That's the thing about men: they may not like to talk about their feelings, but they're usually direct about making their feelings known. If a woman pays attention to what a man is putting out there, she can learn a lot about him—including how he's likely to treat her once the honeymoon is over. And one of the best clues to that is the way he treats his mother.

I liked Mrs. McGraw from the moment Brenda introduced us the night we went on that double date. Her mother was distracted, Phillip being sick in bed and all, but she welcomed me into her home and expressed pleasure that Brenda and I had become friends. I was polite and respectful, as a nineteen-year-old should be toward her girlfriend's mother. But when Phillip and I began dating, I made it a point to go beyond politeness and become his mother's best friend.

It wasn't difficult; Annie Geraldine McGraw is a warm, generous woman, and I could see that Phillip treated her with dignity and
respect. He was always loving, kind, and sweet to her, and I could
see that it was important to him that she be treated that way. Well,
I was not about to get crossways with her—how stupid would that
be? In fact, I truly liked and connected with Phillip's mother, but I
was smart enough to know even then that if I was with a man who
loved his mother—and a man will always love his mother, even if
he doesn't like her—I was going to love her, too.

Now, there are some men who don't get along with their mothers when they're boys, and who don't like or respect their mothers
when they're men. If you're involved with a man like that, he
probably won't have much to do with
his mother, and neither will you. But
when a man behaves in a loving, protective way toward his mother—as
Phillip did toward his mother—he's
sending a clear message about how
he wants you, his wife, to treat her.
So why would you treat your man's
mother any differently than he does?

> But for the most part, a
> mother-in-law is just a
> woman who has invested
> a lifetime of love and
> devotion in a child
> whom she still loves
> with all her heart.

I just don't understand women
who choose not to get along with their mothers-in-law, who speak
negatively about their ways and mock the way they do things. Yes,
I know there are some tough old cookies out there who would try
the patience of even the saintliest daughter-in-law (we've had a few
of them on the show). But for the most part, a mother-in-law is just

a woman who has invested a lifetime of love and devotion in a child whom she still loves with all her heart.

Maybe it's because I'm the mother of sons myself, and know what it's like to see the sun rise in their little faces and know that, if I do my job right, they'll grow up, go off, and leave me wondering how it happened so fast. That's part of the deal, and I accept it wholeheartedly. But I also accept the fact that Annie Geraldine McGraw, a.k.a. Grandma, loved my husband long before I met him, and she loves him still. More to the point, Phillip loves her, and that's all I need to know. I have always adored Phillip's mother; how can you not love a woman who has a heart attack when she sees you crying? And while I started out caring for her because he did, I've come to love her on my own, as a daughter loves a mother.

My mother-in-law has always made it easy for me to love her. But even if she hadn't, I'd love her anyway because I believe it's the right thing to do. The decision to love Phillip's mother was a choice I made, and I made it out of respect both to my husband and to the woman who helped make him into the man I love, the man who has abundantly brought security, peace, and unconditional love into my life.

Phillip may not be perfect, but there's no question that he's the perfect man for me. And I will love him and stay with him and be a good wife to him forever, no matter what. I know this because we had a conversation right before we got married, and we decided that this marriage was forever, that we were never, ever going to divorce. We would never even talk about divorce. We were going to do whatever it took to make the marriage work because we didn't want to live in uncertainty, wondering, is this the day that he walks out? Is this the one thing that's going to make him so angry that he leaves? Or, from his point of view, is this the one thing that's going to make her say, "I've had it—I'm out of here!"? When we both made the commitment and decided that there was nothing, ever, that was going to make either of us leave, it took a lot of pressure off both of us.

You might think it would be the other way around—that a woman and man who were young, still in school, and with little money, might feel anxious that they had sworn to stay together no matter how disap-

> For us, commitment was liberating, not confining, because it promised certainty and continuity that was both comforting and necessary.

pointing things turned out. But for us, commitment granted freedom to the marriage: freedom for both of us to not only be our true selves, but to speak the truth about who we were and what we needed without worrying that either one of us would walk out over a thoughtless remark or a stack of unmailed thank-you notes in a tennis bag. For us, commitment was liberating, not confining, because it promised certainty and continuity that was both comforting and necessary. For me, because of the kind of home I'd come from, it was no less than sacred. And to this day, the most significant aspect of the commitment is that each of us chose to make it, freely and without pressure.

That's why I broke up with Phillip that night in Denton: I was ready to get married and he wasn't. I could have cried and carried on, but emotional blackmail is not my style. (Nor would it have worked; Phillip is immune to psychological manipulation.) No, if we were going to get married, it would be because we both wanted it, no holding back. When Phillip was ready to agree to those terms, I knew we had a deal.

If I sound a bit like a lawyer, it's because I believe that good marriages aren't born, they're made—and they're made over time by an ongoing process of loving, unselfish negotiation. It's funny—people are forever asking me how Phillip and I have managed to be married for thirty years and still be happy. They think we have some sort of mysterious secret; when I tell them that we've done it by negotiating our differences, they look almost disappointed. "Negotiate?" they say. "That sounds so, so . . . unromantic."

Well, hello! Who ever said marriage is romantic? Marriage is about partnership, sharing, cooperation, and compromise. Sure, romance is in there, too, but it tends not to surface unless the other components are in place. And they're not going to fall into place easily and peacefully all the time. Sometimes you have to advocate for yourself in a relationship, which means figuring out what your needs are in a given situation and having the conviction to be honest with your partner about it.

Here's an example. Phillip was in graduate school and I was working for the vending machine company and my sister Cindi invited me to her house for the weekend. She was still married then and the girls were very young, so it was easier for me to go up to Oklahoma—she lived not far from the Texas border—than it was for her to come down to my place. So I called Phillip and told him that I was going to visit my sister for the weekend and I invited him to come along. We weren't married yet, and, between his classes, studying, and teaching assistant job, I didn't see him that much. So I thought it would be fun to hang out with my sister and my nieces for a few days. And he said, "Sure, I'll go."

About an hour later he called back. "I've got to thinking," he said, "and you know what? I am so busy and there's so much I can be doing here, and it's not my thing to sit around and visit and have girl time. I know you want to have a visit with Cindi, so why don't you go by yourself and I'll stay behind? You know I love to spend my free time playing tennis on the weekends and I can't do that there, so . . . unless you really want me to go for some reason, why don't you just go do your thing, and I'll stay here and do my thing? We'll see each other when you get back. Okay?"

And I said, "See you Monday."

Sure, it would have been great if he'd said he wanted to spend the weekend with Cindi and the kids. But the truth was, he didn't. He just wasn't big on sitting around my sister's house playing cards and catching up on family news—things that I like to do—when he could be home catching up on his work, playing tennis, and doing things that *he* needs and likes to do. (The truth is, he wouldn't have wanted to sit around his own sister's house any more than he wanted to sit around mine.) He wasn't putting me down or letting me down; we were only dating at the time, after all, and he was under no obligation to accompany me on a trip whose sole purpose was for me to visit my family. Nor was he implying that I should not go and instead remain in town to be with him. He was merely asserting his preference for the weekend and being honest with me about how he would rather spend his time. It had nothing to do with me, and it had everything to do with him and what he needed to do that weekend to feel responsible, studious, and satisfied with himself.

Now, I know many women would be hurt if their boyfriends turned down an invitation to spend a weekend at their sister's house. They'd work it out in their heads that he didn't really love them, or didn't like their families, or didn't care about their feelings, when they should have been thanking the guy for being honest enough to tell them how he really felt. I actually felt relieved that Phillip told me he didn't want to go, because if he'd come along and been miserable, it would have ruined my weekend.

I wanted to tell this story because when Phillip told it to an interviewer a few months ago, he made it sound as if he refused to go with me because he wasn't big on family—which is, of course, not the case. He never refused to go; in fact, he offered to come along if I really wanted him to. What he meant to say was that he wasn't big on spending the weekend chatting with my family when he had work of his own to do at home—a big difference. So I wanted to set the record straight on what he said and what he meant, and what happened, which is that I went to Cindi's for the weekend, Phillip didn't, and we saw each other when I got back. And I'll always be grateful to him because, by being honest about what he wanted to do, he liberated me to be honest about my preferences, too. And I have been, throughout our marriage.

Just because Phillip and I came together as a couple doesn't mean that we love all the same things. I never understand it when I hear a woman say she's not going to do something she enjoys because her husband won't do it with her, because that means you have to give up part of yourself for as long as you're married. As I said earlier, you're not the same person as your husband; why expect him to like all the same things you do? I love girl time. I love spa days. Phillip wouldn't go to a spa for the day if you held a gun to his head, but he encourages me to do it (go to the spa, not hold a gun to his head). To this day, he urges me to go see my sisters when he senses I'm missing them. He is supportive of anything I want to do that brings me joy, and I am supportive of anything he does that brings him joy.

That's why I insist that he play tennis every day. I still get up in the morning and pack a bag with everything he needs so he can play tennis on his way home from the studio. And he does, every single day that the weather is good (and in LA, it usually is). He's always played tennis after work, and I've always encouraged him to do it.

Over the years a lot of people have said, "I can't believe that it's okay with you that he goes straight to the tennis court for two hours after work." And I always say, "Who am I to tell him he can't do that?" I mean it: he works hard all day, and afterward he needs to work out and sweat and breathe and get rid of his stress. He wants that. That's who he is, and I don't want him to give up an important part of himself because he's married to me.

In a marriage, you have to do what works. We have always eaten dinner late—eight o'clock or later—because Phillip gets off work, plays tennis for a couple of hours, comes home, showers, and only then do we eat. When the boys were little, I never put them to bed early. Women used to think it was odd that I kept my boys up so late. I had friends who put their kids to bed at six or seven o'clock every night, but Phillip would never get to see the boys if I did that. It was important to me that our sons have time with their father every day, so I had them take naps at five o'clock and woke them up at seven-thirty, right before Phillip got home, so he could play with them for a while. Then we'd have dinner together and I'd put the boys to bed at ten or eleven o'clock. That all changed when they started school and had to be up early, of course; but when they were little, I kept them up late because that's what worked for us.

I am not saying that parents across America should keep their preschoolers up late at night. That's what worked for us, so that's what we did. It's not what Dr. Spock was recommending at the time, but he didn't live at our house so he didn't know what was best for us. I did, and that's what I chose to do.

As I said before, it's all about doing whatever it takes to make your partner happy. That is true for husbands and wives alike, but I'm focusing on the wife's part of the deal for obvious reasons. Phillip never told me he wanted the kids to be awake when he got home because that would be invading my motherly turf—something he has never done. I don't think he ever changed a diaper or woke up in the middle of the night with a crying child because that's the way I wanted it. He did wake up once and wander over to Jay's crib when he was crying and I shooed him back to bed because his job was to work during the day to support the family; mine was to care for the family so he could focus on work. That was our agreement when we got married and we were both satisfied with the terms.

Phillip takes his work very seriously—that man loves working more than anyone I know—and I take my work seriously, too. Phillip has never complained about being the sole breadwinner in our family, and I have never felt resentful, put-upon, or exploited because I was responsible for the childcare and housework: those are things that I am good at, and things I love to do. Had I felt overwhelmed or unhappy at any point I would have renegotiated the terms of our agreement. But I have always felt content in the role I chose to play in this life and this family—even when times were hard—because my husband has always shown his appreciation for what I do.

> Nothing means more to a woman than when her family lets her know they appreciate all she's doing for them.

Appreciation is a big component of a successful marriage, and I hope that every underappreciated woman who reads this will circle that last sentence with a Day-Glo marker and put it where her husband or kids can see it. Nothing means more to a woman than when her family lets her know they appreciate all she's doing for them. And every woman does a lot: whether she's a working mother or home full-time, it's the rare woman who isn't the heart of her home, and her worth is beyond reckoning. I know plenty of women who did not choose, as I did, to make full-time careers of raising their families—a lot of them work on the *Dr. Phil* show—and who work demanding, full-time jobs and then go home to husbands and children and housework galore. No matter how much money they bring in, there's nothing more important in these women's lives— or in any woman's life—than feeling she is special and irreplaceable to the people she loves.

Phillip has always made me feel special. From the time we were dating, he has always known just what to do to surprise me, please me, and remind me that he appreciates what I bring to his life. Nowadays, he tends to express his gratitude rather lavishly—he surprised me with a brand-new Mercedes convertible for Christmas last year—but in spite of such over-the-top generosity, he knows that it doesn't take a lot of money to make me feel special.

Back when we were dating, he'd be studying for exams at his place when all of a sudden he'd appear at my door, present me with a cupcake, and say, "I told myself that when I read and outlined two more chapters, I could come over and see you and bring you this." That was how he paid himself off to get through his work. Another time he brought me an album by Gene Pitney, a pop singer with a hit called "Twenty-Four Hours from Tulsa," which I liked because I'd lived in Oklahoma as a little girl. I can't remember what I did with that album, but I do remember how special it made me feel to know that Phillip was rewarding himself by coming to see me.

And then there was the time we went to the university bookstore so Phillip could buy a textbook. We were married but still didn't have a lot of money, and I was standing there and on the wall were hanging these crewel embroidery kits in clear plastic display bags. Crewelwork had become popular because it was easy to do and, unlike cross-stitching, you could use longer stitches to make free-form, flowing designs.

This one kit caught my eye. It had a color photograph showing what the finished piece looked like, and it was just adorable: a big wicker chair with a cat on the seat cushion and a bushy fern hanging over it. It was a good size—probably 11" x 16"—so I could make a pillow out of it or frame it and make a wall hanging. Everything you needed was in the package, and I could see little coils of embroidery yarn in orange, green, blue, pink, and gold. Suddenly Phillip was standing there, saying, "Are you ready to go?"

I said, "Oh, look at that beautiful embroidery kit! One of these days I'm going to save up my money and I'm going to get that." And he said, "Yeah, it's cute for sure. Let's go." So we left the bookstore and I remember thinking to myself, *I don't care how long it takes but I'm going to save up and buy that and stitch it because it would look precious in our apartment.* And it wasn't inexpensive— the kit cost about twenty dollars, which was a lot of money back then, especially for us.

About two or three weeks later we're in the apartment—Phillip is studying and I'm doing something in the kitchen—and he asks me if I've brought in the newspaper. This was a little odd, because Phillip had never asked me to bring in the paper before. I said, no, the paper was outside, but that I would bring it in a little later.

"Well, do you think you could you bring it in now, please?" he asks.

And so I say, "Okay, fine." I stop what I'm doing, go out to get the newspaper, then set it down on the table where he's working.

"Well, open it up," he says. I unfold it and start looking at the first page.

"What's that?" he says.

"What's *what?*" Now I'm getting a little impatient.

"That," he says, pointing to a piece of paper on the floor. I figure it must have fallen out of the paper, so I pick it up and it's a note and it says: "Robin: Go outside the apartment, around the swimming pool, and over to the oak tree."

"Phillip, look at this!" I stare at the note and see that it's in this spidery handwriting that I recognize as Phillip's, only he's tried to disguise it.

> The simple act of turning your consciousness away from your own inner world to connect with your partner's is a great gift to a relationship; in fact, it's the essence of relationship.

"Oh my gosh, what's going on?" I say, gasping a bit for good measure. "What if someone's waiting out there and grabs us?" So we go outside and around the swimming pool to the tree and there's a big rock at the base of it with another note peeking out from underneath it. This one says, "Turn to your ten o'clock position, go fifteen steps around the bush and into the patch of ivy." (He was a pilot, you see, and when you're flying a plane you talk about everything being in your ten o'clock position, or your three o'clock position, and the like.)

Phillip sent me on a little scavenger hunt around our apartment building, ten steps here and twelve steps there, around the parking lot and across the lawn, and at the end was that crewel embroidery kit, hidden inside a hedge.

Phillip has been like that throughout our life together. He thinks, *What can I do to make her life fun, happy, and exciting?* And whether he's surprising me with a fifteen-cent cupcake or a fifty-thousand-dollar car, his motivation is the same: to please me and see me excited. And while I confess it's pretty exciting to find a brand new Mercedes in the driveway, it's no more thrilling than finding a twenty-dollar embroidery kit in the hedges when it's from the man you love and it's all you can afford. The fact that Phillip went to all that trouble, writing and planting the notes, hiding the kit, and setting it up in a way that he knew would delight me instead of just saying, "Here, I bought this for you today"—it makes me tear up just thinking about it.

Most of all, there's the fact that he paid attention to what I said in the bookstore that day—if there's a secret to a happy marriage, that's got to be it. The simple act of turning your consciousness away from your own inner world to connect with your partner's is a great gift to a relationship; in fact, it's the essence of relationship. You've got to be willing to put energy into listening to your partner—not just hearing, but really listening—so you can pick up signals he's sending out about what he needs to be happy. And you've also got to be willing to send out some signals yourself that enable your partner to make *you* happy.

I was once talking to a woman who was complaining that her birthday had just passed and once again her husband had failed to give her a pair of diamond stud earrings that she wanted very badly.

I asked her if she had told him that she wanted the earrings and she said, "No, but I shouldn't have to; he should know what I want by now. And besides, I wanted him to surprise me."

"Well," I said, "how can the poor man surprise you if you don't tell him what you want?"

Yes, Phillip surprised me with that embroidery kit, but the only reason he knew I liked it was because I made a point of saying so. I didn't do it expecting him to buy it for me; I had every intention of saving up the twenty bucks and buying it for myself. But I had nothing to lose by saying something, and in doing so, I gave Phillip the information he needed to make me happy, and he gave me the gift of paying attention.

That is something that Phillip and I have always given each other: we pay attention. And while much of what I do for Phillip is obvious—taking care of the children, managing the household, sitting in the audience every day—much of what he does for me is much less visible but no less precious.

A series of events in the mid-1980s made me aware of exactly how precious he is. The first one happened about six months after my mother died. We were living in the old house we'd bought, and Phillip was in private practice. He had just started conducting a seminar he had developed based on therapeutic strategies he was using in his practice. It was one of the first workshops of its kind and brought people together for a weekend to explore, identify, and overcome obstacles they believed were preventing them from living up to their full potential. I thought it might be useful to me, as I was still grieving the loss of my mother and the seminar sounded like fun. So Jay went off to spend the night with a friend and I put myself in the program.

A large group of people had signed up for the session: men and women, individuals and couples, married and single. I took my place among them as Phillip led us through a series of exercises and activities designed to acquaint us with the others in the group and with ourselves. The goal was to help us get in touch with thoughts and feelings lurking just beneath the surface of our social masks— the slick, superficial faces we present to others to hide who we really are.

Phillip never came near me or looked directly at me. He told me beforehand he'd be keeping his distance because he didn't want to appear to be hovering around me, nor did he want to inhibit my ability to respond honestly to the exercises. This was fine with me; besides, Phillip had a team of trained assistants helping him run the session, so there were plenty of trainers to go around.

Phillip announced that we were going to do a letting-go exercise, broke us up into groups and told us to gather in circles and close our eyes. I heard his voice saying, "Search deep, really deep. Get down in there and look in the dark corners of yourself. What regrets do you live with? What do you want to dig out and get rid of?" And he told us to visualize this regret, take it in hand, and then, with an actual throwing motion, get rid of it by virtually tossing it into the middle of the circle.

I was drawing a blank. One of my mottoes is that I never want to live with regret, so I didn't have a ready supply to draw from. Around me voices were murmuring, "I regret never tracking down my biological mother"; "I regret that I haven't been there for my children"; "I regret that I didn't take that promotion."

I remember thinking, *Okay, I'm going to have to throw something in here, but I don't what it should be. What regrets do I have? I regret . . . I regret . . .*

And then it came to me, and I said, "I regret the decision to have only one child."

In truth, Phillip and I had both decided to have one child. When Jay was about two years old we sat down and discussed our options and decided it was best for Phillip to have a vasectomy, which he was happy to do. Now four years had passed, our son was healthy, our income was stable, and on some level I was reevaluating the wisdom of taking the only-child route. I wasn't angry with myself for making that decision, nor did I harbor resentment against Phillip for having had the procedure; the choice felt right at the time. But as I stood there, digging down deep, I thought, *I do regret it now. I regret that decision to only have one child.* And I said it aloud, as we had all been told to do.

That was in spring 1985. A few months later I went to the gynecologist for my annual exam and Pap test. My doctor was a man named Joe Miller, and Phillip and I would sometimes join him and his wife Liz for dinner. So it was both as a doctor and a friend that Joe called the house a few days after my appointment and told me that my Pap smear had come back at level four, which meant that not only were there cancer cells present but they had invaded the surrounding uterine tissue. This was bad, and he wanted to put me in the hospital right away and do a hysterectomy, which would mean removing both my uterus and any hopes I may have had about having another child.

It was a sobering prospect for me, given what I had admitted to myself at the seminar a few months before. I had not said anything to Phillip about my evolving change of heart, figuring I had plenty of time to broach the subject . . . until now. Now I suddenly had no time left at all. I covered the mouthpiece and told Phillip what Joe said, which prompted Phillip to get on the phone and ask if there was a less drastic measure we might try.

This was more than twenty years ago, before women's health was so much of a medical specialty. Back then doctors were much less reluctant to perform hysterectomies than they are today, even on women who were still young enough to have children. I was only thirty-two with many more childbearing years ahead of me, but Joe didn't want to take any chances.

"We can take out the uterus and we don't have to worry about how far the cancer has gone," he said. "You've already got a healthy child. Let's just take the uterus out and be done with it."

"Yes, I understand, but is there anything else we can do that's not so radical?" Phillip said.

"There is something we can do, but it's a long shot," Joe said.

"Go ahead—try us," Phillip said.

So Joe told us about a procedure that would in effect freeze the cancer cells and kill them, after which the doctor would insert an instrument and slough off the dead tissue. They would do the procedure once a week for three weeks, at which point the hope was that all the malignant cells would be dead and gone.

"We could try that," Joe said, "because at the end of three weeks it won't be any worse. Then we'll do another Pap smear. If the level is normal, we'll know it worked. But even if it does work, I'll agree to do this only if you'll agree that we'll do a Pap smear every month for six months to make sure it hasn't come back. Because if it comes back, we're doing a hysterectomy, and you're not going to talk me out of it."

I agreed.

That was at the end of August. Over the next three weeks I went in and had the freezing procedure done three times. By the end of September I was pronounced cancer-free, and had happily consented to going in for a monthly Pap smear. From where I was sitting, it was a very small price to pay for keeping my body intact.

A few months went by and now it was early December. It was about five o'clock and I was at home fixing dinner for Jay, who was six years old and changing into his basketball clothes. He had a game at seven and I liked to feed him early when he was playing. The three of us usually ate together on game nights because Phillip was the coach and we'd all head out to the game after dinner. But Phillip had phoned me a few hours earlier to say he might not make it home in time to eat because he was in Joe Miller's office at the hospital, helping him with a patient.

"What are you doing with Joe?" I asked.

"Well, he's got this patient and he wants me to help talk her out of having another baby," he said.

"What, is she sick?" I said.

"Not really. But she's already got one child and Joe thinks another pregnancy could be hard for her and—"

"Let me tell you something," I said. "If that woman wants another baby, Phillip, you help her get it. You do everything you can to help her. You're a man; you don't know. If that woman knows in her heart she wants another baby, then you help her get it. Don't you be talking her out of it." He was silent for a moment.

"Well, okay," he said, and hung up.

At five o'clock the phone rang; it was a nurse calling from the hospital.

"Mrs. McGraw, I'm sorry but your husband is held up here with a patient. He has instructed me to tell you to go ahead to the game and fill in for him. He'll be there shortly."

This sounded fishy. It wasn't like Phillip to delegate a phone call like that to someone else; if he were really held up with a patient, he would have excused himself, called home and gotten Jay on the line, and explained that he might miss the first quarter but would get there as soon as he could. It was a little scary because my mother had died suddenly just a year earlier, and I couldn't help worrying that maybe something had happened to Phillip. But I told myself to stop being paranoid and get on with dinner. I called some friends whose son was also playing that night and asked them if they might drive us to the game so we could ride home afterward with Phillip.

And so the game starts and I'm filling in as coach for these six-year-old kids and I keep glancing at the gymnasium door, looking for Phillip and thinking, *Where is he, where is he?*, but he never shows up. Now I'm getting very worried and thinking that some-thing must have happened to him because Phillip would never miss a game. And I'm thinking, *This is not good, this is not good at all.*

So the game ends and Jay is wondering where his dad is and I'm worried to death and trying to act all calm and normal. Our friends take us home and as we pull up to see a car in the driveway and I'm thinking, *Whose car is this and why are they here?* I run up the steps and look in the kitchen window and I see Dr. Joe Miller, our friend, sitting at the table, but I don't see Phillip. And I think, *Oh, no, Phillip is dead. That's why Joe is here, because he's on staff and they know we're friends and he's the one they'd send to tell me that something terrible has happened.*

So I walk in with this wild look in my eyes and Joe is sort of smiling at me and I'm very confused because I don't know why he's so happy when my husband is dead.

"Don't worry," Joe says, "everything's okay." And then Phillip walks in from the den only he's walking a bit like a monster, with his legs all stiff and eyes kind of glassy like he's auditioning for *Night of the Living Dead.*

I thought, *Well, at least he's alive.* He was in his work clothes so he couldn't have been in a car wreck or a shoot-out. And he wasn't covered with blood or anything. So I'm starting to breathe more normally and then I see he's holding a gift of some kind. Finally my voice started working again.

"What is wrong with you, Phillip? And Joe, why are you here? What's going on?"

"Don't worry," Phillip says. "Just . . . here, take this." And he holds out the package.

"What's this for? What's going on? Why won't anyone answer me?"

"Just open it, okay?"

So I tear off the gift wrap and find a box stuffed with tissue paper and two little outfits—one pink and one blue—along with two greeting cards. One says, "It's a girl!" and the other, "It's a boy!"

And suddenly I know what's going on: Phillip has adopted a baby girl and boy for me! Joe had recently facilitated a private adoption for someone in his family through a source in Dallas, and now here's Phillip and here's Joe and they've spent the day together in Dallas adopting a set of twins for me. It made perfect sense.

Of course it made no sense at all but that didn't hit me until a second later when I realized that no one in her right mind would let her twins be adopted by a guy wearing a wedding ring who didn't bother to let his wife in on the deal. But for one fleeting, ridiculous instant it seemed plausible that Phillip would do something like that because I'm a twin, and he knew I would have loved to have had twins. And Joe was an obstetrician, so it was conceivable that he might know of a woman who wanted to put her baby up for adoption. Now that I look back on it I have to laugh because of course Phillip and I would have discussed something as major as adopting a child and gone through the process together. But for a split second I'm wondering, *Where are the babies? In the family room?*

And then Phillip says, "If you're wondering why I'm walking

like this, it's because I had my vasectomy reversed today so we could try and have another child."

All I could do was stutter, "You didn't! You didn't!" And then I took a good look at him and saw that he had a bulge under his trousers from a bandage and icepack.

It was true.

And then it all began to make sense. His eyes looked glazed due to the anesthesia, which had taken a long time to wear off, and that was why he missed the game. And that mysterious phone call about the patient whom he was supposedly talking out of having another child—fabricating that story was his way of feeling me out about the situation and giving me a chance to say, "Sure, she's already got one kid, she doesn't need another one." But when I told him he should do everything he could to help that woman get the baby she wanted, he knew I was talking about myself, even if I didn't know it.

I was thrilled and moved and didn't have the words to express my gratitude. But I did find a few to ask my husband a question. "Phillip, how in the world did you know? How did you know I've been feeling like I want another baby?"

"I heard you that night in the seminar," he said. "Your eyes were closed so I knew you wouldn't be distracted by me walking past you, and just as I did, I heard you say something about having only one child. It was the exercise about getting rid of regrets so I knew what you meant. And I knew what I had to do."

You've got to love a man who does something like that. And I do, every day, but never more than ten-and-a-half months later when, on October 21, 1986, I gave birth to our son Jordan, two years to the day after my mother died. Every year I am reminded of my twin treasures, my mother and my son, and I am doubly blessed because I know my mother had a lot to do with Jordan's birth. I can just imagine the Lord saying, "Georgia Mae, here's the deal: you come with me, and two years from now, I'll give your daughter the most perfect, beautiful baby boy. You and I, we are going to give her this baby."

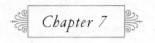

Chapter 7

A Confident Heart

When I'm Right, I'm Right

S omething was wrong with Jay. Every time I fed him, he vomited so forcefully that it shot across the room. I knew projectile vomiting was common in infants but this had been going on for more than twenty-four hours and it was happening every time he ate. I was becoming anxious whenever it was time to feed him. Making matters worse was the fact that I had fed him diluted formula for the first few days of his life, so he was tiny to begin with and now, nearly a week later, he barely weighed more than when he was born.

I took Jay to the pediatrician, an older man who had been recommended to me as wise and experienced, if a bit on the gruff side. He took a quick look at my baby and then turned to me.

"You're a nervous mother, and you've gotten him all jumpy,

too," he said. "He's picking up on your nervousness and now he's too tense to eat. Here, give him a few drops of this before you give him his bottle and it'll relax him." He handed me a small vial of liquid with a medicine dropper attached to the inside of the lid.

"What is this?" I said.

"Something to soothe him, relax him," he said.

"You mean like a tranquilizer?"

"Something like that. Just give it to him and it'll calm him down enough to have a bottle. You should try to relax, too."

I walked out of there thinking, *No, I am not going to drug my baby so he can have a bottle.* The only thing I was nervous about was the fact that something was wrong with my child, and the doctor wasn't doing anything about it.

I called the doctor back the next day and told him that I wanted to bring the baby back in. But he said to give it another day or two.

Two more days passed and Jay was still vomiting. He was looking even skinnier and was starting to act weak and listless, so I called the office again.

"Doctor, you've got to listen to me. Something's very wrong, and I want you to check the baby again," I said. "I know what you said last time, but I know my baby and this has nothing to do with nerves. You've got to see him right away."

There was a gravelly sigh at the other end of the line but he agreed to see Jay in the morning. I put the baby to bed that night thinking, *Relax, Robin—you'll take him in tomorrow. Everything will be fine, you'll see.*

I woke up feeling unusually well rested and then realized why:

the baby hadn't woken me up in the middle of the night to feed him. I felt great for a nanosecond until my rational mind kicked in and I thought, *No, that's not right—it's too soon for him to sleep through the night, he gets too hungry; it just can't be.* I ran down the hall to the nursery.

Jay was lying motionless in his crib except for his poor little belly going up and down as he breathed. He was so weak, he couldn't cry loudly enough to wake me to feed him. He looked as if he were starving to death, which wasn't far from the truth. It was only 8:15 and the doctor's office wouldn't open for another forty-five minutes, but I wasn't about to stand around doing nothing. Phillip had already left for work so I threw on some clothes, scooped Jay out of his crib, then called my sister-in-law Donna and asked if she could come over right away and take me to the pediatrician. I wanted to devote all my attention to Jay and not worry about driving; besides, Donna had three kids of her own and was no stranger to medical emergencies.

We arrived at the doctor's office before he did and I remember pacing in circles around the reception area thinking, *Hurry, please hurry . . . I can't wait, I can't wait.* Then he walked in and I went right up to him with Jay in my arms and said, "There is something wrong with this baby and I'm tired of you telling me it's because I'm a nervous mother. You need to see him right now." He told me to bring him on back into the examining room.

I laid Jay on the table and unwrapped his blanket. The doctor walked over, looked at the baby, and then looked at me. "How long has this been going on?" As if he didn't know.

"What do you mean? I had him in here five days ago and you told me I was a nervous mother and sent me home with tranquilizing drops. I've been calling you all week and you keep telling me to wait another day and I've been trying to tell you that there's something wrong with him." He took another look at Jay and called over his shoulder to the nurse to alert the hospital that we were on our way.

"We have to get him into surgery right away," he said. "I'll explain when we get there." He then headed out to his car and we headed out to ours.

Donna drove straight to the hospital; Phillip met us there. When the pediatrician arrived he said that he believed that Jay had a condition known as pyloric stenosis, a digestive disorder affecting three out of a thousand babies born in the United States. What happens is the muscles in the lower part of the baby's stomach, known as the pylorus, thicken and enlarge, making it impossible for food to empty out of the stomach into the small intestine. As food builds up in the stomach, the baby vomits explosively, expelling everything it takes in and eventually growing malnourished and weak because its body isn't receiving any nutrients.

No one knows for sure what causes the condition; one theory is that the pylorus thickens as a result of an allergic reaction; another theory suggests that during pregnancy, the mother's hormones predispose the fetus to developing the disorder. The doctor said it was a relatively common problem that is far more likely to afflict the first born male child in a family, so even though it is hereditary, any other sons we might have would be much less likely to have the problem. I did not find this particularly comforting; all I could think was, *How can you make this out to be so common when my baby is about to die?*

The doctor reassured us that he could perform a simple operation to open the passage between Jay's stomach and his intestines and, after a couple of days in the hospital for observation, he could go home and would be just fine.

"So this has nothing to do with me after all, does it?" I said. For once, the man looked just a tad embarrassed.

"No, Mrs. McGraw. It had nothing to do with you." And I made a mental note of how, when someone knows he's wrong—and knows *you* know he's wrong—he starts showing a little more respect for you.

They began prepping Jay for surgery. They were having trouble inserting an intravenous line because he was dehydrated and his little veins had collapsed, so they started looking for a spot on his scalp. Phillip knew I would not be able to bear seeing a needle in his poor little head, so he suggested they try to put it in his hand. They balled his hand into a tiny fist, found a vein, and tried to insert the needle but it wouldn't go.

They tried again but they still couldn't get it in. I was holding him and he was screaming, but he was so weak that all that came out were squeaky gasping sounds. They said they would try the hand one more time before inserting the needle in his scalp. This time, by the grace of God, they managed to insert the IV.

My poor baby was so weak, he didn't have the energy to cry. He lay in my arms, sobbing and trembling, and I remember thinking,

Of all the things that have happened in my life, this is the worst, the absolute worst.

Once they got the IV in, everyone started rushing toward the operating room. The doctor was walking and saying, "Okay, let's go, let's go." Phillip was on staff, so they let him carry Jay into surgery.

I will never forget watching Phillip walk with Jay toward the operating room. He was holding him close to his chest with his little head up on his shoulder. And as he walked away from me, all I could see was this tall husband of mine with his big, broad shoulders and this little tiny head peeking up over one of them. My heart was pounding in my chest and I heard myself saying, "Oh my God, what is happening? What's happening to my baby?"

> As I stood there, not in the hospital chapel and not in a room but right there in the hall, I gave my child up to God.

As I stood there, not in the hospital chapel and not in a room but right there in the hall, I gave my child up to God. *Lord,* I prayed, *letting go of that baby is the hardest thing I've ever had to do, but I'm letting him go and I'm turning him over to You. Please hold his little life in Your hands, Lord, and, if it is in Your will, please, please give him back to me. Amen.*

That may have been the first time I really turned my life and the life of my child completely over to God. And as I did it, I felt a burden lift from my shoulders and my heart, because I knew my baby's life was in God's hands. I continued to pray as Phillip and Jay walked farther and farther away, and when they disappeared beyond a set of double doors I sat down for an eternity to wait.

Two hours later, Phillip returned and handed Jay back to me. "He's going to sleep for a while," Phillip said, "but he's fine. He's fine."

The doctor wanted to keep Jay in the hospital for a couple of days to make sure his stomach was working properly. They switched him to a diet of soy milk, which is easier to digest than cow's milk and, two days later, he came home.

Most new parents have had an episode like that, a close call that turned out well but was scary for a while. It stays with you because the feelings it provokes are so powerful that they remain vivid decades later, well after the child is grown. What I remember most clearly about Jay's illness is the fierceness of the feelings I had and how they defined me as a mother. It was my calling to take care of that child; I was his mother, and I believed then as I believe now that I was called by God to love and protect him with every breath I had in me.

> It was my calling to take care of that child; I was his mother, and I believed then as I believe now that I was called by God to love and protect him with every breath I had in me.

Most mothers have this knowledge, stronger than intuition or anything in a book. You know your child, you know when something isn't right, and you know that you must do something about it. I had been a mother for less than a month, but there were two things I was sure of: there was something wrong with my baby, and there was nothing wrong with me.

I still get riled up when I think about that doctor telling me I was nervous and had made my baby sick. The man was neither evil nor incompetent, but he was old-fashioned in his thinking and it was easy for him to dismiss me as an overwrought, emotional female. Which was why it was important for me to listen to my heart, speak my mind, and insist that he take me seriously enough to examine my son again.

I learned from that experience, and what I learned was to trust my instincts and not back down when I know I'm right. If I have to make a fuss, fine; if people get annoyed with me, so be it. Ruffling a few feathers is a small price to pay for saving my child's life. And I'm convinced that is what I did that day. I absolutely believe that if I had obeyed the doctor like the good little girl he expected me to be, Jay might have become severely dehydrated, fallen into a coma, and perhaps even have died.

As women, we are trained from childhood to be good little girls, to smile and charm and be agreeable. But acting agreeable is not a virtue when you know in your heart that you absolutely, positively *disagree* with the people around you. If you smile and nod and go along with the crowd—or the authorities—when your heart is telling you otherwise, you are betraying your true self and denying your God-given powers of discernment.

What I learned from Jay's bout with pyloric stenosis served me well a little less than two years later when he had his second medical adventure. I was getting him into his pajamas one night, and he said, "Mommy, I have a headache." I had taken him to have his picture made that afternoon and he had been a bit quieter than usual, which I attributed to shyness. And I remember thinking, *How is this child articulate enough to say he has a headache? Not "Something hurts," or "I hurt," but "I have a headache."*

I took his temperature. It was 102 degrees, so I gave him some acetaminophen and put him in our bed so we could watch over him.

Jay was sick all night, dozing fitfully and then waking up and crying about the pain in his head. I sent Phillip off to work at about seven, and I told him I'd keep him posted. By eight o'clock Jay's headache was getting worse and his fever was up to 104.5 degrees, so I called Phillip's mother and asked her to come over. She was there in a flash and we rushed him to the pediatrician—the same one who had diagnosed his earlier illness. This time he took us straight back to the examining room.

He took a quick look at Jay, disappeared for a moment, then came back with his coat on and said to me, "Call the father and tell him to meet us at the hospital. We're going to go right now. I'll ride with you."

I thought, *This is serious. Usually they tell you to take your time driving to the hospital. When they tell you they're coming with you, it's serious.* I asked Grandma to get Jay dressed again and I ran out to the reception area to use the phone (this was 1981, long before everyone had a cell phone). I called Phillip at work, told him to meet us at the hospital, and the four of us piled into the car and headed out.

When we pulled up to the emergency room, I let out the doctor with Grandma and Jay, told them that I was going to park the car, and drove across the street to the parking lot. I found a spot, locked the car, and started running toward the hospital.

It's funny how certain things stick with you, because I remember starting to run across the street and getting only halfway because I had to stop for an oncoming car. The car slowed down and stopped before reaching me and I glanced up as if to say thanks.

Then I saw the driver, and I froze because I recognized her as a woman whose two-year-old son had died the year before. I am a very aware person; I take in everything and I don't miss much. And I remember all the traffic on the street moving as if in slow motion, and I remember seeing her and thinking, *Why am I seeing this woman? Of all the people driving on this street right now, why should I see the woman whose two-year-old son died last year?*

That encounter had meaning for me. I couldn't have told you what it meant, but a stab of recognition went through me and all I knew was that it meant *something*. Maybe she was there to warn me of the terrible, unnamable thing that might happen, or to remind me to be grateful that my little boy was still alive. Or maybe it was pure coincidence and nothing more. But whoever or whatever brought the two of us together wasn't finished working miracles that day, because something even eerier happened a little later on. But I'm getting ahead of myself.

I found the cubicle where they had taken Jay; Phillip got there a few minutes later. The doctors said they needed to do a spinal tap, which is painful in general and especially dangerous for young children because the patient has to lie very still so the needle can be inserted into the spine without injury. They needed someone to help restrain Jay; Phillip said he'd do it because I knew I couldn't.

I watched as they tied sheets around Jay's body to keep him still on the table. They were going to stick that big needle in his spine, and I ran out of the room and straight to a pay phone to call my father. At that point my mother was working part-time and would have been out but my dad would be home. All I could think of was getting him down there to be with me.

"Daddy," I said, "we're at the hospital with Jay. He's so sick that they've tied him to a table, and they're . . . they're about to do a . . . they're about to, they're about to . . ." And as hard as I tried, I couldn't get out "spinal tap." I don't know if I couldn't think of the phrase, or if I couldn't bear to speak it. I just stood there, hanging on to the pay phone, sobbing and trembling and repeating myself.

"They've tied him to a table, daddy, and they're going to—"

"What? What?" my father said.

"They're doing a, they're doing a . . . "

"Robin, calm down and tell me what's happening."

"They've got him on a table and they have to put this, this . . ."

It was then that I noticed the man sitting in a chair beside me, right by the phone. He stood up and took the receiver from my hand and said into it, "They're just going to do a spinal tap on him. He's going to be fine."

He gave me back the receiver, and I put it to my ear and I heard my father say, "I'm on my way." And I said, "Okay, daddy." And I turned around to thank the man and he was gone.

To this day, I believe that man was an angel, an angel sent to bring my father to me because I couldn't do it myself. As soon as he said those words, "He's going to be fine," a sense of peace and tranquility settled on me, and I was able to calm down enough to talk to my father. My dad cared deeply for Jay and me. I needed him badly right then, but could not summon the words to communicate clearly. I had not even been aware that anyone was sitting near me; he seemed to materialize from nowhere. When he took the phone from my hand, that man was as real as you or I; yet when I turned around and looked for him, he was gone. But I believe in angels. And that was an angel that day.

Jay was diagnosed with viral encephalitis, an inflammation of the brain. He probably got it from a mosquito bite (as I did a year later, an experience that gave new meaning to Jay's understated "Mommy, I have a headache"). He was in the hospital for four days while the illness ran its course—there is no set treatment for this kind of infection—and doctors watched to make sure his heart and lungs continued to function. But the point I'm getting to is that even when a child is out of danger and in a reputable hospital, a mother still has to be vigilant and do what is necessary to take care of him.

Here's what happened. Jay was in his hospital bed with an intravenous line in the top of his hand when two nurses came in. One was about fifty years old, bustling and efficient; the other was much younger.

"Hello," says the older woman cheerfully. "This is Sandy. She's a student and we're here to change . . ."—she paused to look at the chart hanging at the foot of the bed—"to change Jay's IV."

"Oh, okay," I said, smiling efficiently myself. I looked at the bag of medication dripping into the line, saw there was plenty left, and thought, *Why do they need to change the IV?* I didn't have the answer but thought that as long as they were disconnecting the line I might as well change Jay into clean pajamas, which was impossible to do when he was hooked up to the IV. I turned around to get his pajamas and when I turned back I saw the young nurse breaking a fresh needle out of a sterile envelope.

She saw me watching her, and I could see she was nervous. I put my arm around Jay and held his little hand still as she removed the old needle. Then she approached with the new needle, which was shaking a bit. She pressed it into Jay's hand and it started to bleed; he started whimpering, and the older nurse said, "Okay, that's fine. Now, when you try again, you need to . . ." and it dawned on me that this was a training session: she was using my baby's arm to teach this girl how to insert an IV.

The poor young woman went to try again but I'd had enough. "Whoa, just a minute—absolutely not," I said. "You step away from my child right now." The young nurse looked at the older one, and so did I.

"Was this really necessary, changing the needle?" I said. No answer.

"This wasn't necessary, was it?" I said. "You're training this woman and you're using my child to do it, aren't you?" Still no answer. Now I was ticked off.

"Both of you get out—I don't ever want to see either one of you in this room again. And you get me whoever's in charge right now." I was shaking. I took some deep breaths to calm down and busied myself with Jay's pajamas. A few minutes later the head nurse came in.

"Is there a problem?" she said.

"There was," I said. "Two women came in here, removed the IV from my son's hand, and proceeded to use him as a pincushion. I would appreciate it if you—you and no one else—would put the IV back in my son's arm. And don't ever send anyone in here again who doesn't know what she's doing."

And let me tell you, I got the best treatment after that. They were wrong—they knew it, and they knew I knew it. To this day I don't know whether it was necessary to replace the needle in Jay's hand. It's entirely possible that the only reason it was removed was to give that student a warm body to practice on. But I let them know in no uncertain terms that I was not afraid of them, and if they wanted to use my baby as a guinea pig they'd have to deal with me first.

Now, I don't want to give the medical profession a bad rap because of that incident. Phillip was associated with that hospital for many years and worked with many dedicated, caring professionals who saved our son's life at least twice. But you have to stand up for yourself. You can't stand by passively and ignore your maternal, womanly instincts in this or any other kind of challenging situation. You can't let somebody go poking around on your baby's arm or leg or anywhere else. Again, you can't let anyone tell you something about anything in your life without thinking, feeling, and acting in accordance with your

> You can't stand by passively and ignore your maternal, womanly instincts in this or any other kind of challenging situation.

instincts and knowledge. It's not about being stubborn, hardheaded or close-minded; it's about listening to yourself and trusting what you hear.

It's not always easy to stick up for yourself. People in authority can be intimidating, especially when they're not accustomed to being challenged. And there's always a chance that you'll raise a ruckus, only to find out you were wrong and end up looking like an idiot. But I'd rather risk looking like an idiot than feel like one for being too intimidated to stand up for me and mine.

I was in another situation like that a few years ago, only this time with Jordan. He was in seventh grade and playing a lot of sports when he came in one night and showed me a little knot-like bruise on his shin. He wasn't sure when he got it and it didn't hurt, so we figured he got it playing football and, since the season had just ended, we decided to wait for it to go away on its own. Then basketball season started and Jordan began practicing after school and competing on weekends. He soon began complaining of pain in his lower back, which struck me as odd for a twelve-year-old kid. I began to wonder if maybe he'd hurt his back during football season and, remembering how Phillip had wrecked his body playing college ball, decided to take Jordan to the orthopedist to make sure everything was all right.

So I took Jordan in and the doctor examined him and said that it's common for active kids his age to experience growing pains— yes, that's what they call them—and when their backs hurt it's because as the vertebrae grow, tiny amounts of gaseous material can get between them and cause discomfort. The doctor offered to do an X-ray just to make sure there was nothing wrong. I said that sounded good, and then had another thought.

"Doctor," I said, "while you're X-raying Jordan's back, would you also please do this bump on his leg?"

"What bump are you talking about?" he said.

"It's not very big," I said, "and it's right here on his shin bone. He's had it for a while now, since the end of football season."

The doctor looked at it impassively. "It doesn't look like anything to me. I'm sure it's just from getting hit a few times."

That's the moment, the intimidating moment when an expert tells you the truth about a situation and you're expected to accept it, thank him, and go away. Except the expert's truth contradicts something deep in your gut, and you know his truth is different from your truth; and you've got to choose between being a good girl and bowing to authority and being a no-nonsense woman who's not afraid to look like a fool when she's acting in the service of those she loves.

I took a breath and spoke. "Yes, but it's been there for at least three weeks now, and if it were a bruise it would be gone by now."

"Maybe yes and maybe no. Some bruises take longer to heal than others, and we don't like to X-ray every little bump that shows up on these kids. You don't want to expose a young boy to too many X-rays, you know."

"Yes, I know," I said. "But I also know that every other bruise this child has had has healed in less than a week and it worries me that this one is taking so long to disappear. So would you please X-ray it, just to be safe? Please?" He looked at me with exasperation but agreed to do it.

I was waiting in the examining room when the doctor reappeared with a serious look on his face. "How long exactly has he had this knot on his leg?" he said.

"He noticed it about three weeks ago but it may have been there longer," I said.

"I am glad I did that X-ray. We have some cause for concern here, so I'm scheduling an MRI upstairs. They're waiting on him, so why don't you take him up?" It didn't escape me that the man said he was glad *he* had done the X-ray, as if it were his idea in the first place, but I had bigger things to worry about.

I took Jordan straight up to the imaging department and they slid him into one of those big MRI machines and told him not to move. I was scared to death, naturally, so I do what I always do in those situations and phoned my husband.

"Phillip, there's a problem with Jordan. His back is okay but I had to beg them to X-ray this knot on his leg and they think there's a mass growing in there—"

"Slow down, slow down—"

"—they're doing an MRI right now. That doctor was such a jerk, Phillip. I showed him the thing on Jordan's leg and told him how long it had been there and he was so condescending, he dismissed everything I said. I had to actually beg him to do the X-ray. And now my baby's in an MRI machine with something growing on his leg."

"I'll be right there," he said, and hung up.

About five minutes later the orthopedist came out of the elevator and walked over to where I was sitting. "Mrs. McGraw," he said, "I just want to take this opportunity to apologize for the way I talked to you downstairs and for dismissing your concerns as unimportant."

Well, this was a switch. I was speechless.

"I understand now that I came off as rude and there's no excuse for it. This is a very serious matter, and I shouldn't have taken it lightly when you brought it to my attention. I should not have been so disrespectful of you, and I apologize."

I was beginning to think I had been teleported to a parallel universe when it dawned on me. "Did you by any chance receive a call from my husband?" I said.

"Yes ma'am, I did."

"Well," I said, "maybe next time you'll listen to a mother when she says she's worried about something, whether you think it's important or not."

"Yes, Mrs. McGraw. I surely will."

Jordan's bump was important but not serious. He had a benign mass growing on his tibia and the orthopedist—who was also a surgeon—was able to remove it. Jordan spent a couple of nights in the hospital; the mass never returned.

> What I am urging is that you become an active participant in the creation and maintenance of your own well-being and that of your loved ones.

What returns for me, however, is the memory of that afternoon, and how a child's well-being was so utterly dependent on his mother's persistence rather than a physician's expertise. It left an indelible imprint on me, and confirmed what I learned when Jay's pyloric stenosis went undiagnosed for so long: you don't have to have a medical degree to know when something is wrong with your kid, and you don't have to apologize to a nurse or a doctor or anyone else for saying so.

I am not urging you to be mistrustful of health workers or hostile toward the medical profession. What I am urging is that you become an active participant in the creation and maintenance of your own well-being and that of your loved ones. Sometimes that requires pushing back. Too many people are content to merely go along to get along.

It's not enough, for example, to show up at the clinic, wait your turn (usually far too long), and spend your three minutes with the physician (or physician's assistant or nurse practitioner) listening passively and filling the prescription you may get on your way out. You have to be fully present at the encounter, which means not just listening but interacting with the person who is treating you.

I make a point of asking questions. If a physician says something I don't understand, I ask what he's talking about. If I have read or heard something that I'd like to have confirmed or debunked, I'll raise the issue. If the doctor seems to be missing something that I consider important, I'll bring it up. And if he—or she—seems to be ignoring something I'm saying or dismissing something I'm feeling, I let him or her know, politely but firmly, that I am a force to be reckoned with. Don't be intimidated because you don't have a professional degree: you don't need one to be knowledgeable about your own body, mind, or family. I am not a doctor, lawyer, or teacher, but that doesn't stop me from reading everything I can get my hands and eyes on, and educating myself about issues that concern me and my family.

Just ask the people at the bank in Waco, Texas, where I had my checking account thirty years ago. Phillip was doing his internship, and I was working and watching our finances very carefully. So naturally I was surprised and dismayed when someone from the bank called me at work one day and said that a check of mine had bounced. I knew it wasn't possible because I balanced the checkbook every month and kept track of every check we wrote and every deposit we made. When you have no money growing up, you pay close attention when you start earning some, no matter how modest the wage. Plus, I had worked at a bank before, so I knew how quickly they would slap a fee on your account if you weren't paying attention.

I went to the bank on my lunch hour and sat down with an account representative at one of those big wooden desks. She told me that I had written a check to a grocery store that the bank had returned to the grocer, unpaid, because our account lacked sufficient funds to cover the amount.

"There has got to be a mistake somewhere," I said, "because there's no way our checking account doesn't have enough money in it to cover sixteen dollars and thirty-seven cents."

"There's no mistake," she said. "You're not the first person to be in this situation; no one ever believes their account is overdrawn. Believe me, it happens all the time."

"Well, it doesn't happen to me." Now I was annoyed. "I'd like to see the records for our account, please, because I know that you should not have returned that check."

"It won't do any good, you know," she said.

"Perhaps not, but I'd like to see them just the same. If you don't mind." She was so haughty and condescending, it ticked me off even more. She disappeared for a while and came out with a computer printout showing all the deposits and withdrawals we had made and all the checks we had written. It was all there in front of me, but it was still wrong.

"This isn't possible, it just isn't possible," I said.

"Well, it is, it is," said Miss Know-It-All. "Look at it. It's obvious, if you'd just accept it." Oooh, she was getting me mad.

"You need to stop right there and quit talking to me like that," I said, "because I know that you've made a mistake—"

"We haven't made a mistake—"

"Oh yes, you have, and I'm going to find it if I have to sit here all day." I asked if I could use her phone, and I called Phillip (I always call Phillip). "Phillip," I said, "I'm sorry to bother you. Did you by any chance withdraw some money from the checking account?"

"No; you've got the checkbook, don't you?"

"Yes, I do, but I'm wondering if you came in to the bank and filled out a withdrawal slip and took money out of the account."

"No, I haven't been to the bank."

"Okay, because I'm at the bank now and they're telling me that I bounced a check for sixteen dollars and thirty-seven cents. I happen to know it's not possible because according to the checkbook we're up over three hundred dollars, so they've made some sort of mistake."

"Well, now Robin, those banks, they know what they're doing," my husband said. "They have computers and they know what they're doing, so it is probably you. You need to go over those records one more time. I think I'm going to have to side with the bank on this one. Look, I'm kind of in the middle of something here, so I'm going to hang up now, okay?"

Well, that was helpful.

I had expected him to say, "Don't worry, I'll be right there," which he often does, as you know. Or he might have said, "Robin, you just stand your ground, because I'm sure you're right." But he didn't. He said he was going to have to side with the bank. I said fine, and hung up on him.

I was on my own. It was me against the bank and I was not leaving until the matter was settled. I called work and told them I was going to be late coming back from lunch. I then turned my attention to the account representative and asked her to please get the records for our savings account. That looked all right, so I sent her back to get another record of this and another record of that and the more I tried to research the problem, the testier she got. She would make comments like, "I wish you would just trust us on this," and "You're wasting everybody's time." The snider her remarks became, the more determined I became to sit in that chair until I uncovered the error. I had visions of the janitor waxing the floor at midnight and me still sitting there, poring over printouts.

It didn't take quite that long. Ten minutes later I found a notation in my checkbook for a deposit that didn't appear on any of the bank's spreadsheets.

"See here," I said. "Three weeks ago I made a deposit of four hundred dollars that isn't listed on your paperwork." She flipped the printout around and ran her finger down a column of numbers.

"I noted it right here in my checkbook, see?" I showed her the credit memo in the check register. "So where is it?"

"It isn't here."

"Exactly. We need to find out what happened on that deposit."

"You never made the deposit, ma'am. You think you did, but you obviously didn't," she said.

"You know what, lady? I made this deposit. I brought it up to that window over there"—I gestured to the other side of the room—"and gave it to that teller right there. So I want you to go back, please, and bring me a list of all the deposits the bank took in that day."

If looks could kill, I would have been in a body bag right there at her desk. She got up and disappeared through a doorway and didn't come back for a long time—fifteen, maybe twenty minutes. Finally she reappeared with a different printout in her hand and an embarrassed look on her face.

"I am so sorry," she said. "You were right. It is our fault." And she explained that they had mistakenly credited my check to another person's account.

I was vindicated. And as tempting as it was to let that woman have it, I exerted admirable restraint. I didn't gloat or look down my nose at her or jump up on her desk and break into a victory dance, which I really felt like doing.

"Well you know, we all make mistakes," I said, "but I knew that I was right and there was no way I was going to leave here until you knew it, too."

"I'm so sorry, Mrs. McGraw. What can we do to make this right?"

"You know what you can do? First you can credit my account for the deposit. Then you can credit me for all the fees you charged me when you returned my check. You can also pick up the phone and call the grocery store and tell them that you made a mistake, that my check is perfectly good, and that they may redeposit it at their earliest convenience. Hand me the phone book and I'll find you their number."

She called the store, explained the situation, and then turned back to me, as sweet as could be. "Is there anything else, Mrs. McGraw?"

"Yes, please. I'd like you to write a letter on bank stationery explaining the check was returned in error and have the bank president sign it just in case there are any questions when I go in there again."

"All right, then—"

"Oh, and one more thing," I said. I was on a roll. "I'd like you to write another letter, please, also on bank stationery, explaining the bank's mistake. And address this one to my husband." And I sat there while she did it.

I wasn't really angry with Phillip. He was very busy doing his internship, and I didn't expect him to drop whatever he was doing and attend to my problems. But just the same, I thought, *I am not going to allow someone to push me around and tell me I'm wrong when I know I'm right*. That was the bottom line: I had enough faith in myself to know that there was no way I had allowed our account to get overdrawn.

You've got to listen to that voice inside you that tells you the truth. It's quiet and steady and certain of its rightness because it comes from a deep part of you, the part of you that simply *knows*. Each of us has that deep inner wisdom that comes from our life experiences, but we don't always trust it enough to obey it. When I obeyed my inner wisdom that day I learned that when I knew I was right, I would take on anything and anybody—and that I would win.

That woman tried her best to push me around and persuade me I was wrong. But I hung in there until I convinced her that my truth was a lot closer to reality than hers. And I'd still be there today if that's how long it took to prove my case, because when I'm right, I'm right.

Now let me make something perfectly clear: I am not saying that I'm always right. We all make mistakes, including me, and there were probably other times when I did have a check bounce because I thought I'd made a deposit that I never got around to making. But in this instance I knew I had brought that check into the bank—we're talking black and white

> You've got to listen to that voice inside you that tells you the truth. It's quiet and steady and certain of its rightness because it comes from a deep part of you, the part of you that simply *knows*. Each of us has that deep inner wisdom that comes from our life experiences, but we don't always trust it enough to obey it.

here—and when you know you're right, you're doing yourself a disservice if you don't stick up for yourself.

It's very important that women not be afraid to stand up for themselves. Too many women are willing to abdicate their responsibility as mature, thinking adults because they have been taught that they should defer to authority, especially when the authority is a man. We women can be a little too quick to abandon our inner wisdom when someone in a position of power contradicts it.

I am not afraid to question authority. I am not willing to give my power away to anybody just because she sits behind a desk or wears a white coat. I believe I am accountable for whatever happens to me and to those under my care, and that this is true for all of us. I believe it is my responsibility to stand up for what I believe is right, no matter how uncomfortable it feels. Moreover, I believe that is what God wants me to do. He blessed me with the intelligence to think for myself and with parents who taught me to trust my judgment, and I believe I would be squandering these gifts from above if I did not put them to good use here on earth.

Stand up for yourself. It isn't necessary to be a bully; you don't have to be mean. But when it comes to looking out for yourself, the one who is ultimately responsible is *you*. And I'm not just talking about medical emergencies and business disputes where the stakes are obviously, glaringly high. I'm also talking about everyday situations when you're not being treated as you would like to be, but you let it slide because you don't want to embroil your family, friends, or spouse in a conflict. There's always a temptation to ignore these episodes, telling yourself that they're no big deal and not worth fighting over when, in fact, you don't have to approach every difference of opinion as a conflict. I learned early in my marriage that sometimes the best way to conquer the other side is to join it.

It's no secret that I don't like being told what to do. As you know from reading this book, I tend to think things through before I take action, and I take responsibility for what I do. Which is not to say that I'm never impulsive; I wouldn't own so many pairs of high-heeled shoes if I thought everything through that carefully. But when it comes to running the household and taking care of the children, I've always considered myself organized and reliable.

So it came as a surprise to me some years ago when Phillip decided that I needed to be on a budget. Jay was in first grade, Jordan was an infant, and we were living well within our means, so this development caught me off-guard. Phillip grew up very poor and I knew that he liked to be clear about how he was spending his money (or, in this case, how I was spending it). He has always said he wants to know where every penny goes because he doesn't want to spend money on something and then six months later need the money and regret that he spent it stupidly.

While I don't spend money stupidly, either, I'm much more likely to say, "Oh gosh, lighten up. Let's have some fun!" If I want something and we can afford it, I'll buy it. So it's probably safe to say that the number-one topic of spirited conversation in our marriage has always been money. Not because I spend money we don't have; I've never done that, and Phillip hasn't, either. But we do have different priorities when it comes to money, a fact that didn't manifest itself until we began to have some.

Up to now it had never been a problem (at least I didn't think it had been). We had a good system: I didn't tell him how to do his job, and he didn't tell me how to do mine. I made all the decisions around the house: when we ate, what we ate, and how I cooked it. I researched everything: neighborhoods, preschools, public and private schools, doctors (yes, I picked them), dentists, music teachers, sports teams—and decided which ones to live in, attend, go to, hire, and play for. I figured out what we needed, and I did 99 percent of the shopping.

I thought all this had been working out very nicely. Phillip trusted me, and I thought I was doing a pretty good job. Then all of a sudden, he comes in and says, "Robin, I think it would be a good idea if we set up a budget."

"A budget?" I said.

"Yes, you know, to keep track of how much money we're spending."

"You're saying 'we,' but I do most of the spending around here. I do all the shopping and I write a lot more checks than you do. I balance the checkbook every month and we seem to be doing just fine. Is there a problem?"

"No, no, there's no problem. I just think it would be good to have some spending guidelines."

Phillip went over how much the mortgage and utilities were running every month and showed me a list he had prepared of how much he thought groceries and clothes should cost, as well as toys for the kids, school supplies, and household extras. "This is what I think you should spend on food each week," he said, pointing to a figure that was about half of what I typically shelled out.

I looked at the neat, buttoned-up little budget he had created. It wouldn't have been so bad if he'd had any idea of what things cost.

"Phillip," I said, "you don't know what I pay for things. I spend about twice as much on groceries as you've budgeted for."

"Okay, fine, then we'll double that amount," he said, writing in the new figure. "But anything that's outside the totals I've written down here, we should discuss."

"I want to make sure I've got this straight," I said. "You're saying that if I need something that's not listed here, that's outside this budget, I need to talk to you about it before I buy it?"

"Yes, that's what I'd like you to do."

"Well then, fine."

You know how I'm always talking about making choices? Well, I'd just made one.

The next morning I called Phillip at work. "Hi, honey. Listen, I just dropped Jay off at school and I'm on my way to get him some clothes but it's not in the budget, so is it okay if I spend $600 for the year's uniforms?"

"Yes, Robin, that's fine."

"Thank you, honey," I said. About an hour later I called him again.

"Honey, hi. Sorry to bother you, but I'm at the nursery and they've got a great deal on perennials for the beds in front of the house. Is it okay with you if I pick up about $100 worth of flowers and plant them in the front yard? I know it's not in the budget but they'd really look beautiful out there."

"Yes, Robin. Go ahead and get the flowers. I'm with a patient right now."

"Oh, okay—sorry."

Later that afternoon I called him again.

"Hi, honey. Remember I told you my brakes were making a funny noise? Well, I'm at the dealership and they're saying it's a good thing I came in because I need new pads. It's going to cost about—"

"Robin, I don't want you driving around with bad brakes. Have them fixed."

"Oh, thank you. Thank you, honey."

That particular budget lasted a day. *A day.* The way I saw it, it was my job to run the house, and I had been doing just fine. I didn't think I needed a supervisor. What I wanted to say to my husband was, "Until I show you that I can't do my job, don't try and tell me how to do it." But I knew if I said that, I'd come off as a smart-aleck. I had to stick up for myself but I had to do it in a way that would work, so I showed Phillip that his budget idea would cost him more in time and aggravation than anything he might save by micromanaging me. By the time he came home that night, that budget was history.

Every woman is different, and what works for me may not work for you. But there is one thing that works for all of us, and that is confidence. There is nothing unfeminine about confidence; in fact, many men will tell you there is nothing more attractive than a woman who knows her own mind and stands by what she thinks. When you are confident, you tell the world that you will not be taken advantage of. You teach the men in your life to treat you with dignity and respect, and you set an example for your children of what a strong, independent woman can accomplish in this world (and what a blessing she is to her husband).

Have confidence in yourself. Trust your own judgment. When you know you're right, don't let anyone tell you otherwise. Don't stop; don't back down. Stand up for yourself and defend what you know is true. If you don't, no one else will.

Chapter 8

THE HEART OF
MY HOME

When I sat down to write this book, I wasn't sure of where to begin; now I don't want it to end. Once I got started, I realized that it's not that different from cleaning out the attic: it's a big job, and you're not sure what you're going to find up there, so you put it off for a while. Then one day you get in the mood and you climb up that funky little ladder and back in time, back into yourself. You open a carton, pull out a rattle, and remember the music it made when your baby shook it. An hour later you're still sitting there with that rattle in your hand and a head full of memories about who you were when your baby held it, who you are now, and everything that happened in between.

That's what writing this book has been like: I have dredged up near-forgotten memories, dusted them off, and found myself living them over again, as if those events happened only yesterday. I have heard my parents' voices and my children's laughter; I have seen Phillip's messy hair the night we met and the awful pixie haircut my grandmother gave me when I was seven. I have smelled the aromatic candles I burn in the house and the pie my mother baked for me the day she died. I have relived moments I thought were gone forever, and they have granted me insight into who I was then, and who I am now.

> Above all things and embracing all things, I am the heart of my home.

Like everyone else, I am not one person but many. I am a daughter to parents no longer living; a sister to four adults who bear scars, as I do, of growing up in a loving but chaotic household. I am a wife to a man whose heart I hold in my hands; and a mother to sons whose lives I hold dearer than my own. I am a sister-in-law, a daughter-in-law, and I am soon to have a daughter-in-law of my own. And above all things and embracing all things, I am the heart of my home.

Aren't all women the hearts of their homes? Whether we live alone or in a household spanning three generations, whether we work outside the home as well as within it or stay at home full-time, it's the women who make sure there's food in the fridge, curtains on the windows, sheets on the beds, and a hug for whoever needs it. With few exceptions, it's a woman's spirit that brings a house its warmth, brightens its shadowy corners, and provides those who live there with a soft place to fall. There are as many ways to do this as there are women: we all have our own unique way of being in this world and creating the joy and warmth that make a house a home.

I have always chosen to cultivate a spirit of happiness in our home. It didn't get there by itself; I made it that way. It is not enough that I am happy in myself; I choose to spread a spirit of joy and fun to the family. If I don't, Phillip and the boys might not have it, and it's exactly what they need.

If I weren't around, my husband would probably work all the time, and he's not the only one: I often hear women talking about how their husbands have forgotten how to leave work behind, let go, and have fun. A lot of these are working women, so they understand how difficult it is to juggle professional and personal responsibilities. Still, they seem to be better at making time for fun than their husbands, and are at a loss as to how to help their husbands do the same. I know what it's like to be married to a man who loves to work, and I'd like to pass on something I've learned: one of the best things women can do to make their husbands happy is to be happy themselves. Phillip cannot stand it if he thinks I'm unhappy about something, and I know it brings a real peace to his life—and to our household—to know that I am just where I want to be, doing just what I want to do.

I like to try to make everything fun for my family. When the boys were little and Phillip and I were going out of town—Phillip traveled a lot to do seminars, and sometimes I would go with him— we would leave them with their grandparents, who spoiled them rotten. Still, just to make sure they didn't miss us too much, I would get little bags and if we were going to be gone Monday, Tuesday, and Wednesday, I'd write "Monday a.m.," "Monday p.m.," and so on. I'd put a little note in along with something fun—a Hot Wheels car, a piece of gum, a sucker, whatever they loved—and they'd get to open them when they woke up in the morning and before they went to bed. That was my way of letting them know that there were times when mom and dad needed to go away together, but that we were always loving them and thinking of them.

I also made a big deal about holidays. In spring, I would buy little napkins decorated with Easter eggs and chicks, write a message on the napkin, and stick it in their lunch boxes so they'd get a loving note from me while they were at school. Every Valentine's Day I would buy red heart-shaped balloons and tie them to their chairs before they came down for breakfast. On their birthdays I took lipstick and wrote messages on their bathroom mirror while they were sleeping, so they'd wake up, go in to brush their teeth, and get a surprise.

I would often try to find ways to surprise them. On the days Jay had a game after school, I would drive out there and take him a hot lunch because the school he went to had no kitchen, and he'd get hungry during the game if he hadn't had a substantial lunch. I would serve the boys' favorite dinner on game days, and surprise them with their favorite dessert. Sometimes I'd bake a chocolate-chip cookie cake (get rolled-up cookie dough, press it into a pan and, presto!), put their jersey number on it in M&Ms, and let them have it when we got home from the game. They loved that because not only did it make game days feel special to them, it let them know that I thought they were special, too.

Of all the holidays, Christmas is the one we celebrate the most traditionally, with a huge, decorated tree, tons of presents, and lots of time together. One of our favorite holiday traditions is to attend yuletide concerts at our church. Sometimes we visit other churches because we love hearing different choirs sing Christmas carols.

But for other special days, nine times out of ten our favorite way to celebrate is to just stay home with a simple dinner; a lot of the time, we don't even give gifts. It's actually quite common for Phillip and me to not give each other anything on birthdays or our anniversary because we express our gratitude for each other all year round.

> That's one thing about men: they love to know that their women appreciate them. Sometimes the best gift you can give your man is the reassurance that his happiness means something to you.

That's one thing about men: they love to know that their women appreciate them. Sometimes the best gift you can give your man is the reassurance that his happiness means something to you. It's good to remember that men have feelings, even though they do their best to hide them.

One Christmas morning many years ago I was opening a gift from Phillip and looked up to see him watching me. He had that look on his face that a man gets when he's done something special for his wife and he can't wait to see her reaction. I tore off the wrapping, lifted the lid, and with a cry of joyful surprise, held up the contents for the whole family to see. It was a black suede bomber jacket decorated with fringe across the front, back, and cuffs and embroidered with red and blue crystal beads and glistening, iridescent sequins.

It was striking, unique, beautifully made, and I didn't like it. I turned to Phillip and he was beaming just the way Jordan and Jay did when they gave me Mother's Day cards they had made themselves. And I thought, *He's so proud at having picked this out for me. He must have thought, "I'm going to go buy her something to wear," and he picked out this jacket and he wants to see me in it, and, oh my gosh, I don't like it.* But I would never tell him that.

"Hey!" he said, his face bright and expectant. "Do you like it?"

"Oh, honey, this is a beautiful gift!" I said, and I threw my arms around him and hugged him. And the fact is, the jacket was beautiful in its own way, if for no other reason than that Phillip had bought it and wanted so much for me to like it.

I displayed the jacket prominently all day and hung it in my closet that night. On several occasions after that, when Phillip called me from the tennis court to tell me he was on his way home, I put on the jacket as if I had worn it that day. And when he walked in from work there I was, wearing the jacket, and his face lit up and I knew I had made him happy. I never said anything about it because I thought that would be too obvious; I just wore it . . . but never out of the house. The funny part is that I would probably love that jacket and wear it today because my taste has changed. The challenge was to find a way of showing my husband that I loved what the jacket symbolized even if I didn't love the jacket itself.

Now, if you're thinking that I wasn't being exactly honest with

Phillip about my feelings that Christmas morning, you're right: I was being genuine, not honest, because to be totally honest would have meant being brutal and hurting his feelings. I've got to tell you: if I had to do it over, I wouldn't change a thing, because it was an opportunity to show my sons that the feelings of my husband—their father—were important to me. As the heart of my home, I believe it's my responsibility to take every opportunity to teach my children that people's feelings matter. It's not that I condone misleading people; I would never mislead someone about anything that really mattered. But we all fib a little; we say good-bye to a friend and tell him we'll see him around when we know we'll see him that night at a surprise party being given in his honor; and we all make believe we haven't bought our kids the birthday present we know they want so much. And don't tell me you haven't told your friend that you like the color she's painted her dining room or the sweater her boyfriend gave her when you think it's the most awful thing you've ever seen. Sparing Phillip's feelings that morning was far more important than being honest with him about how I felt about the jacket.

I always tried to teach my children to be sensitive about other people's feelings. I think it's very important to show compassion not only for family, but for friends and other people as well. I took every opportunity to teach this to my sons, and it always thrilled me when I saw that they were actually learning what I was trying to teach them.

I remember the day Jordan came home from school with a troubled look on his face. "Mom, I really feel sorry for this kid, Sam," he said. "Derek is picking on him. They used to be friends, but now Derek and his friends have decided they're going to make fun of him. They pick on him every day in the classroom, and I really feel sorry for him. Sam didn't even want to come into the lunchroom any more, but I started sitting with him and so he came back in. But it's not just at lunch; it's all the time."

Now, let me tell you about Derek. He was the nastiest kid I've ever met, but his family donated lots of money to the school so the principal and teachers looked the other way. Derek got away with everything. As big a bully as he was, the kids tended to side with him because they knew if they didn't, they'd be his next target.

That night at dinner, Jordan told us about what was going on.

"What's he doing to Sam?" Phillip said.

"He grabbed his arm and told him to pick up his book," Jordan said.

"And what did Sam do?"

"First he ignored him, but then Derek pushed him so Sam picked up the book, threw it on his desk and walked away. Sam didn't want to get in trouble for being in a fight."

Phillip put down his knife and fork and looked Jordan straight in the eye. "If anyone ever puts his hands on you, do not—*do not* be afraid of getting in trouble for protecting yourself. I understand why Sam didn't want to get into a fight, but you need to know right now that you have my permission to knock the crap out of anyone who ever tries to bully you. If they try to punish you or kick you out of school, that's okay; we'll handle that. I'll even call the principal and tell him I've given you permission to kick Derek's butt or anyone else's butt who tries to lay a hand on you. Don't go looking for a fight; I don't want you to do that. But you have my permission and your mother's permission to defend yourself at all times."

Neither Phillip nor I think that fighting is the ideal way to solve a conflict, but we felt it was our duty as parents to make sure Jordan knew that he had not only our permission but also our blessing to do whatever was necessary to protect himself. And I felt it was my duty as a mother to call Sam's mother and tell her what her son was going through. As the heart of her home, she had the right to know. Boys that age don't always come out and tell you what's going on with them, and if she was aware that someone was giving my son a hard time, I'd want her to tell me. Because if I know someone is being unfair to my kid, I'm going to go straight to the person in charge—especially if the someone being unfair *is* the person in charge.

This happened at the end of seventh grade, when Jordan was studying for exams. He wanted to be ready for his English final so he arranged to meet with his teacher every morning between 6:30 and 7:30 during finals week for some one-on-one review of the reading material.

We lived about half an hour away from the school, so we had to leave the house at 6:00 a.m. to get there in time. On the morning of the final, I woke Jordan up at 5:15 and he got himself dressed in black warm-up pants, a clean T-shirt, and tennis shoes. I drove him to school, dropped him off at 6:30, wished him luck, turned around, and headed home. I had just walked in the door when the phone rang. It was Jordan, and he sounded upset.

"Mom, I'm so mad! Mr. Connolly said I shouldn't be wearing warm-up pants, and he made me put on this crappy pair of shorts. They're all wrinkled and they don't fit me and I don't want to wear them but he says I have to." It seems that the assistant principal had come around during Jordan's study session, informed him that his clothes were too casual, dragged him to the lost and found, fished out a pair of khaki cargo shorts, and made him put them on. Now I knew my son, and I knew that he was not going to be able to concentrate on the exam if he had to sit there in a pair of nasty old shorts from the lost and found.

"Jordan, how long is it before your exam starts?"

"It starts second period so . . . about forty-five minutes, I think."

"Don't worry, baby," I said. "I'll be right over with some pants for you."

I ran upstairs, grabbed a pair of jeans from Jordan's closet, and got back in the car. This shorts business made no sense to me. It was a private school, and one of the things we had liked about it was that it had a dress code rather than uniforms. Moreover, the code was implied rather than strictly enforced, and it was common knowledge that the kids could dress more casually on test days, so I didn't see what the problem was.

First period was in full swing by the time I got there, so I went directly to Jordan's classroom. I handed him the jeans, waited while he changed in the bathroom, took the shorts from him when he came out, and wished him luck for the second time that day. Then I tucked the shorts under my arm and knocked on the door to the assistant principal's office.

"Hi, come on in," he said and beckoned me inside.

"Hello, Mr. Connelly, how are you?" I said.

"I'm fine, Mrs. McGraw, and you?"

"Actually, I'm not doing well at all."

"Really? What's the problem?"

"First of all, I want to return these." I reached across the desk and handed him the shorts.

"Oh, thank you. Obviously, Jordan didn't like wearing them."

"No, he did not like it at all. And I didn't like it, either. What in the world were you thinking, Mr. Connelly?"

He looked up sharply.

"Pardon me?"

"My son has been getting up every morning at 5:30 to come to school and work with his English teacher so he can do well on his final. He put on a pair of warm-up pants, which I happen to know are clean because I washed them for him last night. And you found it necessary to pick on his clothing on the day he's taking a final? Why would you choose to make an issue out of a pair of pants—which, by the way, covered more of his body than the shorts you loaned him? I think that was poor judgment, Mr. Connelly. I'm just thankful that I had the time to drive back here and give him his jeans, because you know what? Even without having to wear those shorts, my son is going to have a hard time concentrating on his final after you shook him up like that. And if he fails it, I will demand that you allow him to take it over."

He looked at me, looked down at his desk, and then looked up again. "Mrs. McGraw, you're absolutely right," he said. "I understand; I shouldn't have done it." And I thanked him and left.

I said awhile back that one thing I've learned to do is pick my battles, which is more than this man knew how to do. This is one battle I chose to fight because I thought an assistant principal should have been helping my child focus on his schoolwork, not distracting him from it because of an alleged dress code violation.

I also chose this battle because I thought it was important that the extra effort Jordan had put into preparing for his exam not be sabotaged by someone obsessed with rules. It broke my heart— and made me furious—to think that what Jordan might learn from this episode was that it didn't pay to wake up before dawn and study hard because ultimately his clothes mattered more than his mind. There was also the fact that his teacher had come in early all week to work with him and Jordan had made a commitment not only to himself but also to her to do well on the exam. It seemed important that he be given every opportunity to follow through on that commitment (and his hard work paid off—he did just fine on the exam).

Teaching commitment to our children was a priority when the boys were little, which is why we encouraged them to play team sports. We took team participation very seriously and taught the boys that when a coach takes time to work with you, you owe it to him and to the other kids on the team to show up and do your best. You can't skip practice just because you're feeling tired or you're not in the mood to go; to take up a sport is to commit to it. As it turned out, I had to learn that along with my kids.

I remember the day that Jay came to me and said, "Mom, I want to take tae kwon do." I was pregnant with Jordan and Jay had decided he needed to take up martial arts so he could protect his new little brother or sister.

"Now, Jay," I said, "tae kwon do looks like a pretty tough sport. So what do you say we drive over to the studio and watch a few classes so you know what you're getting yourself into?"

I drove him over there and we watched a class. That's something we always did; we made the boys research something before they took it on, to make sure it was what they wanted to do; once they committed, they were going to do it. Then we went home and the three of us talked about it, and when we asked Jay if this was still something he wanted to do, he said it was.

So we signed him up for tae kwon do lessons, both at the studio and with a private teacher. I drove Jay to his tae kwon do lessons, both group and private, three nights a week. And let me tell you—it's a tough sport. He was only six years old, and he often found himself sparring with a twenty-year-old because all the beginners were together in the same class. It was rough on him (and on me, too, sometimes, when I watched him).

One night Jay came home and announced that he hated tae kwon do and wanted to quit. "It's tough, and they hit you, and I don't like it," he said. After what I'd seen I couldn't disagree with him, so I told him it was fine with me, and when Phillip came home I told him that Jay wouldn't be going to tae kwon do any more.

"You know what," he said, "you're a woman, and I don't expect you to completely understand this, but men are different when it comes to sports. Jay made a commitment to tae kwon do, and that child will not quit. He will not quit."

I was so mad!

"How can you let your son go and get knocked around like that?" I said. "He's so little, and he's getting hurt and he doesn't like it!"

"That may be," Philip said, "but the respect he will have for himself when he finishes is much more important than the comfort he'll get from quitting. If he stops now, he'll never know how good it feels to get through it. The lesson he learns about commitment will be great when he finishes, and I don't want him to quit."

Jay went on to study for four more years and finished with a second-degree black belt, which he would not have earned had I let him quit. So Jay learned a lesson about commitment, and I learned a lesson, too: Sometimes I have to accept Phillip's judgment, even if it conflicts with my own. I said earlier that there are some things that Phillip can't understand because he isn't a woman, and I know now that there are some things I can't understand because I'm not a man. The tae kwon do episode taught me that mothers and fathers offer different kinds of wisdom, and that my fears about Jay getting hurt were not as well-founded as Phillip's desire for his son to earn some self-respect.

Over the years, I have often chosen to defer to Phillip's judgment. As a man and as a father of sons, it was his job to teach his sons how to be men and fathers, and only he could do it, not I. Both Jay and Jordan were likely to head up families someday, and I saw Phillip instilling in them the drive and commitment it takes to stand in the door and protect a wife and children. It was a priority for us to teach our boys what it meant to be responsible, mature men, and a big part of that was teaching them respect for women.

I had the perfect opportunity to teach Jay that respect when he was fifteen. He was a sophomore at an all-boys high school and their all-girls sister school was hosting a big dance that weekend. A girl named Christy, whom he'd met at a previous school function, had invited him to escort her to the dance, which was a couple of days away. Jay was studying for finals when I heard the phone ring; then I heard him saying, "Hello. Oh, hi. Oh, okay. Not really, no, I can't talk right now, I'm studying. Well then, see you." He sat back down with his books and I casually walked by.

"Who was that?" I said.

"It was Christy."

"What did she want?"

"She called to see if I had any questions about the dance and talk about the color of her dress or something. You know, I wish I didn't even have to go." He was annoyed that she had interrupted him, and I knew I had to set him straight.

"Jay honey, let me tell you something about girls," I said. "First of all, Christy has spent a lot of time getting ready for this dance. She thought long and hard before she decided whom she wanted to go with her; she picked you, and she's very excited about that. She's spent a lot of time choosing her dress and planning how she's going to wear her hair. You're her guest, and now she's called to tell you the color of her dress—probably to help you pick out a matching corsage—and you act like you don't even want to go with her. That's not fair. In fact, it's rude.

"You need to call her back right now and show her you're excited about this dance. You need to show her the respect she deserves for choosing you to go with her. Because I guarantee you that she is not feeling very happy right now.

"And Jay, let me tell you something else about women: when it comes to men, women never forget. If I were you, I'd be nice to this girl because someday, she just might own the company you want to work for. And I promise you when you walk in for your interview, she will remember how you treated her, and you don't want to lose a job when you're thirty because you didn't act like a gentleman when you were fifteen.

"And let me tell you something else: girls talk. If you don't treat her right, she'll tell all her friends how mean and rude you are. And they'll think twice before they ask you to be their date, or agree to go out with you if you ask them.

"You agreed to escort this girl to her dance, and you should do it with pride. And even if you never want to go out with her again, you should still be her friend. Because afterward, you want her to tell her friends, 'No, we're not dating anymore, but let me tell you something, girls—he is the nicest guy, and I will always be his friend.' Don't ever forget that, Jay. Trust me—I'm a woman, and I know."

I had said my piece. Jay went to the phone, called Christy back, and said all the things he should have said the first time.

There are certain things that only a woman can do, and one of them is teaching her son about women. I wanted Jay to know that it wasn't enough to treat a woman with respect; he also had to treat her with compassion. Women and men often see things differently, and I wanted my sons to know that when they deal with a woman, they would do well to try to see things from her point of view.

It's not always easy to see things from your partner's point of view; but it's something I've consistently tried to do in my marriage. If Phillip and I get along well, it's not because we agree on everything; it's because we both make an effort to understand why the other is thinking, feeling, or acting a certain way. After thirty years, you get to know a man pretty well, and I know that if Phillip and I aren't seeing eye to eye, it's not because he isn't looking at the situation carefully. It's because he's seeing it differently than I am.

Years ago, I knew a woman who lived in a big, beautiful house that I absolutely loved. It was high up on a hill and had wonderful views, and whenever I visited her I'd think to myself, *Now, this is a gorgeous place—I sure wouldn't mind living here.* She and I were talking one day, and she told me she wanted to sell it. I got all excited, thinking, *Gee, maybe . . . maybe.* We had been wanting a bigger house and this one would give us the space without the inconvenience of having to build. I couldn't stop thinking about it, and when Phillip came home I told him that Leigh was putting her house on the market and I wanted him to see it.

So we went and looked at the house. Phillip really liked it and I really loved it. I was already picturing our furniture in the rooms and designing window treatments and imagining the meals I could cook in the gourmet kitchen. The one downside was that the asking price was more than what we had spent on our current house, so we were going to have to decide whether or not the financial angle made sense.

When we got home I went on and on about how much I loved the house and how great it would be for the kids. Phillip listened patiently, then looked up and spoke. "You know what, Robin," he said, "I'm going to try to buy that house for us. But if I get into dealing for the house and they don't take what I offer, the deal is over, and I'm really concerned that I'm going to upset you and you're not going to be happy. But you need to know I will not risk more than we can afford for that house just to make you happy. I want you to be prepared for that. I want you to have the house. But I'm really afraid I'm going to upset you if I have to come back and say, 'We can't make a deal,' because I'm not going to risk any more than I know I can afford."

He was gazing at me intently with this worried look on his face and I thought, *What a precious man. Here he is, doing his job to protect our livelihood and our family, and he's still concerned about disappointing me.* I walked around to where he was standing, wrapped my arms around his waist, and laid my head on his back.

"Where am I right now?" I said.

"You're right behind me," he said.

"That's right," I said. "And don't you ever forget it."

I felt him exhale and relax in my arms.

We ended up not buying the house on the hill. The deal wasn't right for us, and Phillip thought it best to let it go. And as much as I liked that house, it was easy for me to let it go because I knew that if Phillip didn't think it was right for our family, it wasn't meant to be, end of story. Nothing—no thing—could be more precious than my trust for my husband and my belief that he had, and has, our family's best interests at heart.

Believe me, I'm a girl who enjoys her stuff. I love having beautiful things, and wearing pretty clothes, and living in a gracious house in a lovely part of town. But these are only possessions; as long as my husband and I can have true joy in one little corner of our house, all the stuff surrounding it doesn't matter. It doesn't matter where we live: we once lived in a place that wasn't much bigger than my closet is now, and if we had to, I could move back to that apartment and be very fulfilled (a bit cramped, maybe, but fulfilled).

> *Don't worry, Phillip. Don't ever worry about disappointing me because I am right behind you. I trust you, and I know that you're going to make the right decision for our family. I'm on your side; I'll always be on your side.*

What matters to me is the way I felt Phillip relax when I told him I was right behind him. I felt a peace about him at that moment because he knew what I meant: *Don't worry, Phillip. Don't ever worry about disappointing me because I am right behind you. I trust you, and I know that you're going to make the right decision for our family. I'm on your side; I'll always be on your side.*

⌒

I never dreamed that I would write a book, and yet here we are, nearly at the end. Now that we've gotten here, I feel even more grateful for the opportunity I've been given to reach out through these pages and touch other women's hearts. For that is how women are: we connect with others first with our hearts, then with our minds. And writing this book has made me even more aware of the women who have touched my heart and mind, and, in so doing, nurtured my soul.

There's my blessed mother-in-law, whose sturdy, constant strength and love eased the anguish I felt when my beloved mother died. Grandma Jerry is in her eighties now, and of all the gifts she's given me, perhaps the greatest of all is her relentless affirmation of my importance in her son's life. She validates me as a wife, and not only does that make me feel good, it also shows me how to be the kind of mother-in-law I want to be—and that's no small thing when your son is engaged to be married, as mine is. I am absolutely thrilled that Jay picked Erica to be his wife, and I'm going to make sure she knows every day of her life how much I appreciate that she is the one he picked, just the way Grandma Jerry has always done for me. When Phillip and I first got married, his mother would always tell me, "If there's ever a fight, if there's ever a divorce, I'm going with you." If she was ever annoyed with something Phillip said or did in relation to me, she'd always say, "Phillip Calvin"— like every other mother on the planet, she'd use his middle name when he was in trouble—"Phillip Calvin, you'd better be nice to her!" I'll always be grateful to this warm, wonderful woman who has always been loving to me, especially when I needed it most.

And then there's my sister Cindi, whose courage and grace in the face of unspeakable suffering have inspired me with awe. Cindi and her boyfriend were driving to the airport early one morning when a maniac on an overpass dropped a jug of sulfuric acid through the windshield of their car, studding her with glass, catastrophically burning her face and body, and shattering her life. My poor, dear sister was horribly burned over vast portions of her face and body, and her recovery included ghastly episodes of debridement, when her burned, dead skin would be sloughed away from the raw, living tissue beneath it. Cindi would return from these sessions in utter agony, looking as if she had been flayed alive, and I'd wonder, *Why, Lord? Why Cindi?* Why did this happen to this loving, gentle soul, a divorced woman who had raised three daughters and worked two jobs to put them through college and pay for their weddings?

Even today, more than five years later, it's hard for me to discuss the event without wanting to scream and shake with rage about the injustice of it all. But Cindi does not. My amazing sister chooses to see the experience not as a vicious attack against her but precisely for what it was: a random, barbaric act directed at everyone in general and no one in particular by a human being with a profound indifference to human suffering. Cindi knows there is nothing she could have done to avoid or prevent the catastrophe; it was out of her control. She believes that as much as she has suffered (and she has, horribly), there are people who suffer more than she, and for just as little reason. She never felt sorry for herself or expressed grief over her disfigurement. She never cursed the person who did this to her—although, Lord knows, the rest of us did.

This will give you an idea of the pure goodness of my sister's soul. A few years after the attack, Cindi and I appeared on *Larry King*

Live. Her memoir had just been published and Larry, an old friend of Phillip's and mine, suggested she and I come on the show.*

Sitting opposite him at that little desk, I could tell from the look in his eyes that he was devastated for Cindi. Under the unforgiving glare of television studio lighting, he looked at Cindi's scarred face and asked, "Do you ever think, Why me? God, why me?"

Cindi sat quietly for a moment before speaking.

"No, I've never thought that, not once," she said. "If I asked God, 'Why me?' it would mean that I thought it should have happened to someone else. And I could never ever wish this on someone else."

What an amazing woman—what generosity, what love, what strength! Above all, what grace. Not once did she blame God or express anger that He had done this to her. A lot of people would do that, but not Cindi. She never believed that God meant for this terrible thing to happen, for that would have meant she believed she deserved to suffer. This is a prime article of faith both for her and for me: God is there to love us and give us strength. I was proud of her for not caving in to despair and for choosing forgiveness instead. In so doing, she reclaimed her life from horror and insisted on her God-given right to live out her time here on earth.

When I think of my sister's extraordinary grace, I am reminded of God's continuing and eternal presence in our lives. I said at the

* You can read my sister's harrowing and inspiring story in *A Random Act* by Cindi Broaddus with Kimberly Lohman Suiters (New York: William Morrow, 2005).

beginning of this book that I believe we were put on this earth to enjoy lives of joy and abundance. That is what I wish for Cindi and myself, and what I wish for you and for all women. My wish is for you to perceive, as I do, the presence of God within us and around us and feel the love He feels for us all. I have total peace in my heart because I know I can turn to God at any time and ask for help. I know I can. That's why before I get out of bed every morning and before I go to sleep every night, I thank God for all that He has blessed me with.

There will always be people who want to tell you who you should be and what you should do, but no one can tell you how to live your life because there is no one quite like you. Look inside yourself with open eyes and see who's really in there—not your mother or your father, not your husband or your children, but *you*. Go deep, really deep, beyond the labels of wife and mother, daughter and sister, until you find the essential woman inside, the woman God created. See her, embrace her, and honor her by insisting on your right to choose the life you are meant to live.

My hope is that you will see your life as I see mine, as a vast array of choices that can bring you closer to the person you long to be. My dream is for you to bring into your life whomever you cherish and whatever you desire by deciding, as I have, precisely who you are and what you need to be happy. Your life is waiting for you to claim it; it's all in the choosing. May you choose wisely and well.

An Invitation

Now that I have shared my story with you, I invite you to share yours with me. Each of us has a story to tell and I would love to hear yours. Please go to www.RobinMcGraw.com and click on "share your story."